John Weeks

UNPOPULAR CULTURE

The
Ritual
of
Complaint
in
a
British
Bank

THE UNIVERSITY OF CHICAGO PRESS

CHICAGO AND LONDON

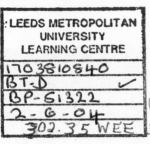

John Weeks is assistant professor of organizational behavior
at INSEAD, Fontainbleau.

The University of Chicago Press, Chicago 60637
The University of Chicago Press, Ltd., London
© 2004 by The University of Chicago
All rights reserved. Published 2004
Printed in the United States of America

13 12 11 10 09 08 07 06 05 04   1 2 3 4 5

ISBN: 0-226-87811-2 (cloth)
ISBN: 0-226-87812-0 (paper)

Library of Congress Cataloging-in-Publication Data

Weeks, John.
    Unpopular culture : the ritual of complaint in a British bank / John Weeks.
        p. cm.
    Includes bibliographical references and index.
    ISBN 0-226-87811-2 (cloth : alk. paper) — ISBN 0-226-87812-0 (pbk. : alk. paper)
        1. Corporate culture—Case studies. 2. Business anthropology—Case studies.
    3. Employee morale—Case studies. I. Title.
    HD58.7 .W334 2004
    302.3'5—dc21

                                                    2003010649

Contents

v

Acknowledgments

In writing this book, I have incurred many debts of gratitude for the help I have been given and the kindnesses I have been shown. The first of these is to my wife, Suzanne, and my children, Andrew and Sophie. They have endured my absences, both physical and mental, with precisely the right amount of impatience: any more and I would have started to worry; any less and I would have started *really* to worry. Families are often acknowledged last (but never least). Having waited so long for this book to be done, however, mine should not have to wait until the end of these acknowledgments to read my expression of deepest thanks for everything that they have done.

My gratitude goes out to my parents for their inspiration and encouragement and not least for the hours of time that they both spent, Mom especially so, editing draft after draft of the manuscript. There is not a page in the book that is not better because of their efforts.

John Van Maanen was another indefatigable reader. My teacher and mentor, John taught me everything I know about ethnography and set for me by his example the highest standard of academic craftsmanship. He guided me with patience and wisdom as I struggled to find my voice.

As our paths crossed at MIT or INSEAD, I had the good fortune to receive valuable assistance with the book from Ian Edwards, Martin Gagiulo, Arnoldo Hax, Herminia Ibarra, Ray Johnson, Bruno Paulson, Leslie Perlow, Andrew Pettigrew, Holly Raider, José Santos, Ed Schein, Michael Scott Morton, and Jean-Claude Thoenig. They were each there with different forms of help at different times during the gestation of this book, and I am grateful for it. My INSEAD colleague Charles Galunic deserves special mention for his tireless support, inspiration, and unflappable good humor even when I ignored his advice, which was seldom. At MIT, my research was funded by the Delta Project.

Without the anonymous reviewers at the University of Chicago Press, this book would have been done too soon and not well enough. Whatever its remaining faults, thanks to them it is more clear and more insightful. At Chicago, the wisdom, patience, and irrepressible enthusiasm of Doug Mitchell, my editor and this book's midwife, made it a pleasure and privilege to work with him.

Finally, there are many people in the Bank who deserve my thanks for sharing with me so generously their time and their wisdom. Although the opinions expressed below are mine alone and any errors of fact or analysis are my responsibility, the study would have been impossible without their help. Not wishing to compromise their anonymity, I will thank them in person and mention them here by initials: KS, PL, SB, GC, DJ, DJ, AR, CS, and the rest of Team 2, BF, PM, RM, BK, RR, RK, JR, NL, RD, BH, DW, VY. A special note of thanks goes to GRW, whose gentle and effective style, openness to learning, and love for the Bank taught me much about leadership and decency. The Bank and I are lucky to have found him.

When I think of those who, through their generous efforts on my behalf, have made this book a possibility, I cannot help but recall the opening words of Boswell's *Life of Johnson:* "I am at last to deliver to the world a Work which I have long promised, and of which, I am afraid, too high expectations have been raised." It is not by chance that I find in the dilemmas he faced those of the ethnographer in general and this ethnographer in particular.

1

uNpopuLar cuLture

Cultures change in ways which some regret
and which please others—sometimes in ways
which seem to nobody's liking.
—Ulf Hannerz

Few management theories—indeed, very few theories in any branch of the social sciences—have much impact on the world that they purport to explain. Some do, however. Some alter the very fabric of the world in which we live, changing how people think and perceive in countless, if sometimes unexpectedly subtle, ways. The theory of organizational culture is one of these. Born twenty-five years ago in organizational sociology as the heir to such earlier studies of the informal side of organizations as Whyte (1955), Jacques (1951), Dalton (1959), Roy (1959–60), and Crozier (1964), the idea that there is culture in organizations passed through adolescence as a management fad and has since matured into a part of the common sense of corporate America and Britain. Indeed, after *Paramount Communications, Inc. v. Time, Inc.* (1989)—which set an important legal precedent by recognizing Time's right to spurn a merger with Paramount because of the possible threat of such a union to Time's distinctive culture—it has become a matter of law. Organizational culture is no longer a theory or a metaphor or a fad; it is a fact of business life. People in organizations now routinely talk about their culture and form opinions about it. And it is here that we find the greatest practical consequence of a quarter century of research about organizational culture. People in organizations now have one more thing to complain about—their culture.

This is not quite the impact that anyone intended, but it was, I would argue, inevitable given the way in which organizational culture entered the public domain. As consequences go, it may not sound very grand, but it is no less interesting for that in what it reveals about the new lay ethnographers of the firm.

This book is about unpopular culture. It is about what happens, and what does not happen, when an organization does not like its culture. It is based on the ethnographic study of one such unpopular culture, the British Armstrong Bank (or BritArm).[1] No one in BritArm, from the chief executive down to the junior clerks, has a good word to say about that organization's culture. Never once during the fieldwork that I conducted in BritArm did I hear it mentioned in a positive context. There were none of the claims common in some organizations about the culture making for an interesting and pleasant place to work or serving as a competitive advantage. Indeed, in BritArm, very little positive is said about *any* aspect of the Bank. Negativity, on the other hand, is common. The Bank's managers and employees complain that it is too bureaucratic, too rules driven, not customer focused enough, not entrepreneurial enough, too inflexible, too prone to navel gazing, too centralized. And, it is added, too negative.

BritArm takes self-deprecation to levels extreme even by British standards. As I describe in detail in chapter 2, in a year when the Bank made profits of £1.6 billion—an increase of 61 percent on the year before—even the announcement of these figures was cast as bad news. Loyalty to the Bank, however, is high, and the same complaints regularly met with bonhomie when heard within the organization are decidedly unwelcome when coming from voices outside it. It is understood that one's dirty laundry is not to be aired in public and, for that matter, is not really to be washed at all. Even though the Bank has spent large sums on repeated (and sometimes overlapping) programs of culture change, the common wisdom holds that managers and employees come and go, assets are acquired and disposed, the organization is periodically restructured, jobs are redefined, and processes are redesigned, but "the Bank hasn't really changed in three hundred years."

To say that something is unpopular is to say two things. The first is that people express an opinion about it. The second is that this opinion is not

1. *British Armstrong* and *BritArm* are pseudonyms. Just as this book was going to press, I received permission to use the real name of the Bank. After considering the matter for enough time to realize that the choice is, indeed, a devilish one, I have uneasily decided to continue to use the pseudonym. This is partly to help protect the anonymity of the people in the Bank who were so generous to me with their time and confidence but partly also to reaffirm my own commitment to the broader, sociological themes and purposes of my work. While this work tells a business story, it is one that I am convinced transcends that of the specific organization that I studied.

A careful reader who is knowledgeable about British banking (or who has strolled the High Street of virtually any village or town in England) may well be able to guess the identify of the organization. For this reason, it is worth my noting that no real names are used in the text and that I have taken some care to disguise identifying features and locations within the Bank.

favorable. For a culture to be unpopular, then, its members must have made public sense of it; they must have arrived at some idea (more or less shared) of what culture is and come to some characterization of their culture in particular. This sense, this idea, this characterization, can be called *lay ethnography*. An unpopular culture, then, is distinguished by the presence of lay ethnography and by that lay ethnography being evaluative and negatively so. Not all cultures will have lay ethnography. Culture, after all, deals with much that is taken for granted and, thus, passes without notice. Further, not all lay ethnography will be negative. Some of the stories that people tell themselves about their culture are purely descriptive; many are self-aggrandizing. However, the fact remains that organizations are likely incubators for negative lay ethnography. This is because there is an influential machinery, a popular literature with associated business school pedagogical materials and with a management consulting industry behind it, whose business it is to create the conditions for unpopular culture.

The practitioner-oriented literature on organizational culture rose to prominence with the publication in 1982 of *In Search of Excellence* by Tom Peters and Robert Waterman (for a genealogy of this literature, see Barley, Meyer, and Gash [1988]). Combining management theory and consulting experience with a study of sixty-two of what they considered to be America's best-run companies, Peters and Waterman (1982, xiii) identified culture as being responsible for the success of these companies and argued that organizational cultures as excellent as theirs are "as rare as a smog-free day in Los Angeles." Well written, well timed—appearing just as American unemployment hit its worst level since the Great Depression and after a glut of books extolling the wonders of Japanese management had left American readers with an apparent appetite for homegrown role models (Micklethwait and Wooldridge 1996, 82)—and well marketed, *In Search of Excellence* sold over a million copies in eleven months and became the first business book to appear on the *New York Times* best-seller list. It helped establish the burgeoning genre of self-help manuals for managers, and it followed the successful rhetorical strategy typical of self-help of all kinds: it created awareness of a topic area; it persuaded readers that they had a problem in this area; and it suggested solutions to this new problem. Equally typical of the self-help genre, it proved more successful at the first two tasks, raising awareness of the issue and heightening discontent around it, than it did at the third, providing concrete solutions.

Roughly two decades after *In Search of Excellence*, the literature on organizational culture has still not delivered on its promise of telling managers with any certainty how they too can use culture to create pleasant, passionate, and profitable organizations. But it *has* had influence: it has succeeded in making organizational culture a part of the socially constructed reality of corporate America and Britain. Pick up any edition of the *Wall Street Journal* or the *Economist,* and you will find literal and unself-conscious reference to the cultures of organizations. Moreover, it does not stop there. By now, to find mention of organizational culture, you can just as easily turn to *USA Today* or the *Evening Standard* or simply turn on the television. *Organizational culture* (and its synonym, *corporate culture*) has entered the lexicon of American and British popular culture. Awareness has been raised.

Packaged with the idea of organizational culture have been exemplars of organizations with excellent cultures. These are meant to heighten readers' discontent, to show them what culture can be and can achieve. Like the figure of the supermodel adorning the cover of a diet book or an exercise tape, however, these exemplary organizational cultures are largely unattainable. This is primarily because these organizations did not achieve their precious cultural qualities by following the advice given in books or by consultants. In fact, it is not clear that they actually achieved those qualities at all. Given the claim that the advantages bestowed by the right organizational culture are enduring, it is embarrassing that studies examining the subsequent performance of the sixty-two companies identified by Peters and Waterman found it to be more average than excellent (Clayman 1987; Ramanujam and Venkatraman 1988). More generally, although the basic messages of this literature have not changed much in twenty years (e.g., Collins and Porras's more recent best-seller *Built to Last* [1994] says little that contradicts *In Search of Excellence*), the companies used to exemplify them have had to be changed several times along the way as corporate fortunes and reputations have waxed and waned. This has proved to be a boon to the publishing industry as it shortens the shelf life of these books and means that old ideas can be resold, seemingly indefinitely, wrapped in ever new examples. The need for a stable of ever new examples does, however, call into question the validity of the claims made about the cultures described in previous editions.

Not only are exemplary cultures less timeless than they appear, but their beauty and shapeliness may also be merely a trick of the light. The cultural descriptions that inform the practitioner literature are typically based on interviews with executives, company publications, and third-party accounts. More detailed organizational ethnographies, such as Van Maanen (1991) and Kunda (1992), have shown that, behind the glossy facades that these sources present, the cultures as experienced by those who live in them can be quite different. And there is a large academic literature devoted to bashing the "seductive promises" (Martin and Meyerson 1988, 94) of practitioner-oriented writing on organizational culture as "slanted and biased application[s] of the concepts" (Meek 1988, 454) "rooted in a distorted theoretical focus" (Young 1991, 90) and so forth. Organizational ethnography and critical organization theory, however, are less read and recounted in organizations themselves than is management self-help, so what those who live in organizations are left with is the idea of culture—a vague and uncertain idea of culture at that—and a set of impossible ideals cast as role models against which they are told to form opinions about the organizational cultures in which they themselves are immersed. It is no wonder that organizations acquire a cultural inferiority complex. The very way in which organizational culture has entered the public domain has planted the seeds of unpopular organizational culture.

In spite of this, both the academic and the practitioner-oriented literatures on organizational culture have systematically ignored the possibility of unpopular culture. The literature aimed at practitioners tends to imply that strong cultures (i.e., those that are persistent and widely shared) are, by definition, well liked by organization members. Peters and Waterman (1982, 77) are typical, noting: "The excellent companies are marked by very strong cultures, so strong that you either buy into their norms or get out." Less desirable and even dysfunctional organizational cultures are not excepted from the rule that cultures persist because they are popular. The longevity of dysfunctional cultures is explained by the fact that they are overvalued by organization members who, because of either arrogance, complacency, or nostalgia, are blinded to, or in denial about, the need for change. The key to changing culture, then, is to overcome this satisfaction with the status quo—in other words, to make the culture unpopular. As one widely cited guide to organizational culture says: "When members of the current culture are at least open to change, it is almost miraculous what . . . change can be brought about just by listing desired norms, because members often start acting out the new norms immediately after they are discussed" (Kilmann 1985, 366). Unpopular culture is, in this view, not just rare; it is inherently unstable.

The academic literature is more cautious and critical in its claims, but it suggests, by omission, that unpopular culture does not exist. Roughly speaking, there are three stances that have been taken toward lay ethnography in academic writing on organizational culture. The first, and most popular, has been to ignore it. In part, this simply reflects differing empirical agendas, but, in some cases, it also derives from a theoretical stance that emphasizes those parts of culture that are taken for granted by members of the culture. Schein (1992, 11–12), for example, argues that the essence of culture is a set of shared basic assumptions and notes: "We tend not to examine assumptions once we have made them but to take them for granted, and we tend not to discuss them, which makes them seemingly unconscious. If we are forced to discuss them, we tend not to examine them but to defend them because we have emotionally invested in them." Lay ethnography is, thus, defined away either as not touching on the essence of culture or as being rare and predictable—and, in either case, uninteresting. Negative lay ethnography is ruled out.

The second stance has been to critique the positive lay ethnography found in some organizations as reflecting corporate propaganda that is at best misleading and at worst dangerous. For example, in an ethnography of one of Peters and Waterman's original "excellent" companies, Kunda (1992) described the hidden side effects of the constant need to express positive feelings about the organization and its culture. These included overwork and burnout for those whose feelings were consistent with the carefully codified, authorized view of the organization's culture and confusion, a loss of authenticity, and a feeling of exclusion for those whose feelings were not so consistent and had to be repressed. In other words, Kunda found the dysfunctional effects of the cultural prohibitions against negative lay ethnography in organizations lauded for their exemplary cultures.

The third stance toward lay ethnography has been to examine the views of members in subcultures within organizations who do not share the positive or neutral views of the organization's culture held by the majority. In some cases—for example, in the bank described by Smith (1990)—this is an elite subculture made up of executives who have decided that, for strategic reasons, the organization's culture needs to be changed but who face resistance from middle managers or employees who view the existing culture more favorably. In other cases, the negative lay ethnography comes from members of deviant, marginal, or minority subcultures who are excluded from participating fully in the purported benefits of the organization's dominant culture and who create identities for themselves within the organization by simultaneously embracing and opposing that culture (for examples, see Martin [1992]). This duality, of expressing loyalty and dislike at the same time, is very similar to what I observed in BritArm. But what has not been considered is that persistent negative lay ethnography need not be restricted to elite or subordinated subcultures, that it may be widespread and may be, if you will forgive my using the phrase, part of the popular culture of the organization.

It should be clear by now that *unpopular culture* is not the opposite of *popular culture*. The opposite of *popular culture* is *high* or *elite culture*. The adjective *popular* has four meanings, and they are all relevant to this discussion, although *unpopular* is the antonym of only one. According to the *Oxford English Dictionary* (2d ed.), the word *popular* may mean (1) "constituted or carried on by the people," (2) "intended for or suited to ordinary people," (3) "finding favor with or approved by the people," or (4) "prevalent or current among, or accepted by, the people." It is this last sense that Berger (1995, 19) has in mind when he refers to popular culture as a "redundancy" because "without at least *some* currency (i.e., popularity) culture would become idiosyncrasy or a curiosity." The word *unpopular* is the antonym of the third sense and means "not possessed of popular favor." It is the first two meanings, however, that animate sociological debate about popular culture and that give popular culture its dual sense of culture made *by* the people (or *folk culture*) and culture made *for* the people (or *mass culture*).

This distinction between popular culture as folk culture and popular culture as mass culture captures the argument in the sociological literature over whether the people are best thought of as active producers of popular culture, through acts of either creation or selection, or as passive consumers who are offered no real choice and, thus, have popular culture imposed on them. If popular culture is something made *by* the people themselves, then it is legitimate to see it as a possible expression of autonomy from the official culture prescribed by elites and as an authentic source of opposition to and liberation from it. If, on the other hand, it is made *for* them, then it is better seen as a form of diffuse social control that ensures the continued reproduction of the established order by pacifying the masses and systematically denying them a view of alternatives to current arrangements. If it is made by the people, then popular culture's (sometimes) unifying effects can be seen as an expression of shared values and beliefs that bind diverse interest groups. If it is made for them, the same phenomenon looks to be homogenization.

Although both these extreme positions—popular culture as purely folk culture and popular culture as purely mass culture—retain their adherents, it is the complicated theoretical ground between them that has proved most fruitful in studies of American and British popular culture writ large (for reviews of this work in sociology and anthropology, respectively, see Mukerji and Schudson [1986] and Traube [1996]) and that is most useful for the present study. This middle ground is a contested one where people are recognized as active in their selection and use of particular modes and forms of popular culture but where attention is also given to the cultural apparatus that shapes the variety of legitimate cultural resources made available to them.

The resulting picture is exemplified by Willis's (1977) ethnographic description of twelve working-class schoolboys in an area of Britain that he refers to as "Hammertown." These "lads" disdain their studies and oppose the authority of their teachers and the norms of the school by bending the rules at every opportunity and by maintaining a stream of humor, banter, and aggressive sarcasm. Willis shows that their rebellious attitudes have the twin unintended consequences of committing these boys to unskilled and unrewarding jobs and of preparing them for that life. Their rejection of the formal socialization into the middle-class values of the school turns out to be an informal socialization into the working-class values of the shop-floor culture where they are headed. This channeling of working-class boys into working-class jobs could not be more effective if it were the school's manifest function. But, here, it is the act of opposition to the school, and to the established order for which the school stands, that performs the task of reproducing that order.

Willis's study is instructive for the present one because, as Giddens (1984, 289–97) notes, by virtue of contesting the authority relations in the school, the lads actually acquire more knowledge about the social system than the conformist children do. Furthermore, the discursive forms that characterize the boys' behavior—the "pisstakes," "kiddings," "windups," and so on—are expressions of this knowledge about, for example, the bases of the teachers' claims to authority and the points at which those are weakest, the exact limits of the insubordination that will be tolerated, and the sorts of spurious justifications that will be adequate if insubordination is taken too far. In other words, they constitute a running commentary about the school culture, a form of lay ethnography and one expressed largely in negative terms. The parallels between the Hammertown classroom and the BritArm banking hall are obviously imperfect (for one thing, the school's teachers do not join in the "piss taking" and "winding up" the way the Bank's managers join in their employees' chorus of complaint). But the same fundamental question that Willis asks of the discursive forms that he hears is one that we must ask of the modes and forms of the unpopular culture heard in BritArm: To what extent and in what manner—in both intention and effect—do these discursive forms serve to reproduce the culture that they critique, and to what extent do they serve to stand in opposition to it?

The answer to this question lies in the cultural competence required to complain effectively about the culture in the Bank and in the sanctions that deter the misuse of complaint. It lies in the ways in which the different types of negative expression about the culture are themselves culturally patterned. To be socialized into the Bank's culture is to come to know not only the way things are done around here but also the way they are complained about. It is to learn not only the official ideology of the organization but also the right and wrong ways to account for it, derogate it, diagnose it, and deprecate it. As Goffman (1974, 575) says: "When we are issued a uniform, we are also issued a skin." Although the skin of cultural disaffection and role distance is accepted as all the more authentic because the uniform of ideology seems artificial, it is just as much a cultural provision. As I argue in detail in the chapters that follow, the cultural norms and prohibitions surrounding complaint in BritArm ensure that, for the most part, far from provoking changes in the culture, legitimate complaint serves to reinforce the culture. Cultural complaint is neutered by the cultural norms that regulate its appropriate use.

To understand the relation between culture and complaint, we must distinguish between four different types of negative expression found in BritArm and elsewhere that reflect different attitudes and intentions of the speaker and have different uses and effects on audiences within the Bank: derogations; deprecations; accounts; and diagnoses.

Derogations are put-downs. Exemplified by the sort of good-natured complaints that we might make to each other about the weather, they are complaints in a broad sense, but they are not calls for any sort of action on the part of the audience. Rather, they are a way of drawing people together through allusion to shared experience.

In contrast, *deprecations* are complaints that express a desire for some kind of redress. Thus, they have the potential for provoking change. However, there are in BritArm strict norms of tact and discretion regulating deprecations, norms that have the effect of making clear, direct deprecation rare. I describe the ways in which the ambiguity between the various types of negative expression is used—with varying degrees of success—politely to disguise deprecation as derogation or diagnosis while preserving its message.

Accounts are explanations of unanticipated or untoward events or behaviors. Unlike criticisms, which draw attention to whatever is untoward, accounts attempt to deflect attention away from it. What is interesting in an unpopular culture like BritArm is the way in which good news is as likely as bad to be unanticipated or untoward and, therefore, to require explaining. An example is the announcement of the Bank's profit figures mentioned earlier.

Finally, like accounts, *diagnoses* are explanations of problem situations. Unlike accounts, however, which seek to justify or excuse the situation so as to make it seem less problematic, diagnoses are analyses of the problem to determine what caused it. Diagnosis is patterned in BritArm by taboos concerning blaming others for problems rather than accepting responsibility oneself. Of course, this bank is no exception to the general rule that blaming others for problems is a highly useful, and occasionally even honest, mode of diagnosis. It is invaluable, therefore, to develop the considerable cultural competence required to be able to blame others or, sometimes even better, to blame the target that cannot talk back and that everybody already agrees is at fault for much else: the culture.

To complain about the Bank's culture is to display affinity with it, not alienation from it. You must know the culture well and be a part of it to be able to complain about it and get away with it. In fact, you must complain about the culture to be a part of it: the sanctions against complaining too little, and being seen as too stiff, too stoic, or just too strange to be completely trusted, are as real as those against being too negative. These rituals of complaint—for that is what they are—do have their uses. They offer legitimate means of bonding and blaming and, occasionally, back stabbing—if not universal human needs, certainly important operations for achieving success in organizational life. What is more, they are a mechanism of self-positioning. They provide breathing space within what might otherwise be a suffocating culture, space where, according to Goffman (1961b, 139), "the individual constantly twists, turns, and squirms, even while allowing himself to be carried along by the controlling definition of the situation." They are a way of displaying one's personal stance toward the organization and its culture, a way of positioning oneself in its landscape of overlapping subcultures and in its status hierarchy. They are a way of asserting one's individuality that is accepted as individual and authentic because it masks cultural conformity and constraint with the bluster of cultural complaint.

When we talk about rituals and masks, we need to be clear about one thing: their efficacy does not depend on anyone being naive or being fooled. The disguise can be seen through, but it must still be put on. To return for a moment to an earlier example: complaining about the weather oils social interaction only if there is agreement that the weather is poor (this agreement is, by the way, culturally bounded and need not be universal: I come from sunny San Diego, where it is often said that you can spot the natives because they are the ones complaining about the weather); it will fail to work if it is clear that the complainer has little idea or interest what the weather is like at the moment and is simply (desperately) trying to make conversation. In the same way, for complaint about the culture to be effective in bonding or blaming or self-positioning, it must be, to use Bourdieu's (1990, 126) term, *misrecognized* as a valid and genuine complaint. Misrecognition implies active symbolic work on the part of both the speaker and the audience to maintain the pretense that is required by the ritual. It is tempting to summarize this symbolic work as, "I pretend to complain about the culture, and you pretend to care," but this captures only half the story. The complaints are real, as they must be, just as the audience must see the complainer as deserving of the redress ostensibly requested by his complaint. It is merely that no one involved has any expectation of that redress being forthcoming or even being desired.

In this sense, complaints in the Bank can be compared to cockfights in Bali. In his classic description of the Balinese cockfight, Geertz (1973a, 443) quotes Auden as saying that "poetry makes nothing happen" and notes that the same is true of the cockfight. That is, although the spectacle of "a chicken hacking another mindlessly to bits" looks like a competition for status among the men with their cocks, it turns out to be exactly that: something that *looks* like a competition for status. No matter how glorious it is to win a fight or how humiliating it is to lose, no one's status really changes as a result of a cockfight. Real rivalries and hostilities are activated—they must be to produce the thrill of risk, the despair of loss, and the pleasure of triumph that Geertz argues are essential for the cockfight to be effective. But, as the Balinese peasants themselves know, it is just play, it is only a cockfight, and what it effects is not a status reordering or even a reinforcement of the current status ordering. Instead, Geertz claims, "It provides a metasocial commentary upon the whole matter of assorting human beings into fixed hierarchical ranks and then organizing the major part of collective existence around that assortment. Its function, if you want to call it that, is interpretive: it is a Balinese reading of Balinese experience, a story they tell themselves about themselves" (448). It is lay ethnography.

The cockfight offers its (human) participants excitement, diversion, and a chance to affirm ties of kinship and friendship. But Geertz's claim is that these are not enough to explain why the Balinese find it so *interesting.* To understand that, we must consider the "sentimental education" that it provides about status in the culture. What the cockfight teaches about status is not what it reveals most easily: who has won; who has lost; who is up; who is down. This literal level of commentary about status is irrelevant because the results of the competition have no implications beyond the cockpit. The interesting lessons that the cockfight offers—first and foremost that status is a matter of life and death—are those that are not told but displayed.

Similarly in BritArm, the rituals of complaint reveal much about the organization's culture, but not usually in the literal claims that the complaints make about the culture. These all too seldom go beyond parroting the popular wisdom about what an "excellent" culture should be like: thus, BritArm is too bureaucratic, not customer focused enough; too inflexible, not entrepreneurial enough; and so on. Rather, the interesting lay ethnography comes in the form of what the choices of complaints, the styles of complaining, and the reactions of audiences (both at the time and later, as stories of complaints are told and retold) *display* about the culture: specifically, about status, hierarchy, and the exercise of power; about subcultural boundaries and group identities; about basic assumptions concerning what it means to be British, what it means to be a banker, what it means to be a banker in BritArm, and what it means to serve British banking customers. And, of course, about the norms of tact and discretion that are strict even by the standards of a country known as "the land of embarrassment and breakfast" (Barnes 1985, 101). Taken individually, each complaint reveals as much about the complainer and the audience and how they position themselves vis-à-vis the culture as it does about the culture itself. As an ensemble, the complaints dramatize the culture for the lay ethnographers of the firm who are both its actors and its audience (and also for the so-called professional ethnographer watching over their shoulders).

So complaining about the culture in the culturally acceptable ways should not be seen as an act of opposition to that culture. Rather, it is a cultural form that is useful for several reasons and that has the effect of enacting the very culture that it ostensibly criticizes. This is not to say that, when people complain about the Bank being inflexible, they do so inflexibly or that, when they complain of too much bureaucracy, they do so bureaucratically—although ironies such as these are favorite anecdotes within the Bank. It is, rather, to say that the performance of a complaint and the reaction to that complaint display and, if the complaint is effective, reinforce certain cultural norms, beliefs, and assumptions. These include, for example, the beliefs that precision is more important than efficiency (making a customer wait is one thing; getting his balance wrong is quite another); that money is not like other commodities in the temptation and opportunity there is to steal it; that the sort of people who are attracted to work in a bank like BritArm prize security over advancement, comfortable routine over challenge or change. When taken together, these norms, beliefs, and assumptions produce the macro-level phenomena of bureaucracy, centralization, and inflexibility that the popular view of organizational culture teaches us to disparage and that are complained about in the Bank. In other words, complaints reinforce the assumptions that produce the very thing being complained about.

There is the danger of overstatement here in that not all complaint is neutered in its opposition to current cultural arrangements. There is always the possibility for heretical complaint, for complaint that is, by the standards of the culture, illegitimate. This possibility is not, however, easily realized. It is hard to be heard over the din of innocuous complaints, and, when you shock people sufficiently that they hear you, they are likely to refuse to listen because you are being rude and possibly dangerous. It is here that power figures importantly in the analysis. Not everyone has equal influence over the provision of meaning in the organization, and, in general, but with important exceptions, those higher up in the hierarchy (i.e., those at the "Centre," in Bank parlance) have a greater ability to shape how the culture is viewed and to change what is considered legitimate and illegitimate, orthodoxy and heresy. This power is never absolute, however, and the influence seldom sure or straightforward. The messages of this cultural apparatus—and the plural is important here since it seldom speaks with one voice—can become distorted and their impact diluted as they are interpreted and appropriated by their audience. What is more, those with the greatest ability to reshape cultural norms and assumptions may be those with the least interest in doing so, especially since ritual complaint usefully serves to euphemize their power. We see elements of each of these factors when examining the Bank's failed culture-change programs and the cultural implications of other changes in the organization. It may not always be true that, the more people complain in BritArm, the more the culture stays the same. But it does seem that, the more things change, the more unpopular they become.

To sum up: The consequence of raising awareness about organizational culture and presenting a model of what that culture should look like is less a creative tension that inspires change than it is the provision of a new cultural resource that people will appropriate for their own—culturally specified—uses. Ultimately, the impact of the collision between management theory and popular culture has not been to lead us to the promised land pointed to by management gurus or to the brave new world feared by their critics. Instead, it has been more modest, if more insidious: to produce a new form of discontent that plays out differently in each organization and that reveals more about the culture than it changes directly. To say more than this, to put flesh on the skeleton that I have provided here of culture and its discontents, requires reference to descriptions of actual practices and experiences, and it is to this task that I turn in chapter 2 with a cultural vignette that sets the stage for what follows by giving a glimpse of the unpopular culture in action.

2

AN iLLuſtratioN

The dogs bark, but the caravan moves on.
—Arabic proverb

Wednesday mornings in the British Armstrong Bank are reserved for Communication Meetings. All across England, the Bank's branches (twenty-two hundred in 1994) open a half hour late, at 9:30, so that managers and staff can convene without the worry of customer interference. Likewise, back office and Head Office departments stop work for the half hour and gather together to discuss issues that have arisen in the past week and to reflect on the challenges of the week ahead. A time-out from the busy-ness of the workweek, the Communication Meeting is ostensibly an opportunity for the whole branch, office, or department to share ideas, air grievances, and compare notes. It is a chance to bond.

At least that is the idea. In practice, that idea has too little structure to suit the tastes of many in the Bank. Senior executives, nervous that the time might be wasted, have weekly briefing packets sent to managers outlining what they are to communicate to their units. Unit managers—many of them unsure of how best to use the time and culturally unable to take (read *waste*) a valuable half hour each week for unstructured discussion and reflection—are only too happy to receive the instructions. They are even happier to receive the videotapes that periodically accompany the briefing packets. These give senior executives a chance to speak directly to all staff and relieve managers of the responsibility for filling all but a handful of the thirty minutes. In short, they subvert entirely the espoused intent of the meetings.

Uniformly of high polish, the briefings and videos are routinely derided by management and staff alike. Any feelings of pride or gratitude in seeing CEO Michael Cole expound the Bank's vision or hearing BBC

14

newsreader Michael Burke announce improvements to the Bank's systems are either absent or left unexpressed. Instead, mannerisms are mocked, clothing critiqued, errors highlighted, managerial claims loudly disbelieved, and executive waffle snorted at. Those managers who choose to read the briefing notes verbatim rather than use them as guidelines for improvisation often have a hard time doing so with a straight face. Managers regularly preface the meetings with apologies for the material and typically join in the good-natured fun that follows.

Communication Meetings do serve a bonding function. They bring the people of an office or a branch together in a traditional way practiced by the English since the Hundred Years' War: by busying "giddy minds with foreign quarrels," as Shakespeare's Henry IV put it (*Henry IV, Part 2*, 4.5). The common enemy in this case is not France, or even a competitor, but BritArm itself. Each Wednesday morning, and countless other times throughout the week, local loyalties are strengthened through shared affirmation of gentle contempt for the Bank. Alienation from the Bank as a whole promotes identification with particular parts of it.

I was only dimly aware of this on the morning of Wednesday, 3 August 1994. Two months into my fieldwork in BritArm I was in the participation phase of my participant-observation. I was acting as a *doer 1* at one of the Bank's Securities Centres, a regional back office processing center. Along with the more senior clerks—called *doers 2*—we doers 1 processed the paperwork necessary to perfect guarantees, mortgages, and mortgage debentures taken by the Bank to secure lending. We checked that charge forms and title documents were in order, that insurance and ground rent were paid up to date, that property valuations had been obtained, and so on. In turn, the assistant managers checked every aspect of our work: *perfection* is the operative word when perfecting securities. In the unlikely event that the Bank had to rely on a piece of security in court, I was told repeatedly, every i must be dotted, every t crossed.

With a staff of over one hundred, the Securities Centre was deemed by its manager, Tom, to be too big for one single Communication Meeting. Instead, he held the meeting in four shifts. Besides castrating the idea of Communication Meetings as important opportunities for the entire unit to come together, this left the Centre short-staffed for much of the morning, an inconvenience that—along with his evident dislike of public speaking—led Tom to cancel the meetings as often as possible. But there was little chance of this particular meeting being canceled. The Bank had announced its interim results the afternoon before, and the meeting would be its chance to put its spin on the numbers. Tom had received his briefing packet. As instructed, he had filled a flip-chart with columns of numbers comparing the 1994 year-to-date figures with those from 1993.

He stood at the front of the basement staff room and joked around as those of us in the ten o'clock group filed in for the third Communication Meeting of the morning.

To the untrained eye, the results seemed exceptionally good. Pretax profits for the first six months of the year had risen to £767 million, an 83 percent increase on the £419 million figure the year before. Bad debt provisions had fallen by 47 percent, and the Bank was reporting a 14 percent increase in its dividend. The trained observers of the British press, however, responded to the results with a cacophony of conflicting criticism. Some newspapers were furious. The Left-leaning *Daily Mirror* had this to say about "piggy banks":

> This is the season when the banks report their profits and we can see where the money they rip off from their customers is going.
>
> Yesterday it was the turn of BritArm, which has made 82 per cent more than a year ago. While still planning to shed 4,200 jobs as it axes branches around the country.
>
> So customers will get an even worse service for their money. There is little we can do about it. One bank is as bad as another.
>
> They are no longer interested in helping private customers or small businesses. They just want to transfer our cash into their profits.
>
> If it happened to them, they would call it robbery. ("Piggy Banks" 1994)

Other papers, such as the more staid *Financial Times*, expressed disappointment with the results: "Yesterday's figures leave room for doubt about BritArm's grip on costs. This is [especially] true of UK retail banking where trading profits fell by 5 per cent and the bank itself admits that further cost cutting is needed. . . . Presumably BritArm is happy to let costs rise as the business grows. But it urgently needs to show that its investment can earn a decent return" ("The Lex Column" 1994). Depending on how you looked at them, the results were either too good or not good enough. Either way, they were bad news. The Bank's response to this (not uncharacteristic) bit of bad press? Agreement.

Reading from his briefing notes, Tom laboriously explained why, despite appearances to the contrary, the results were troubling. Although the technical discussion glazed the eyes of many in the audience, the argument echoes the analysis of the *Financial Times* and can be summarized as follows. The results announced were for BritArm Group as a whole, not just BritArm UK Branch Banking (UKBB). Much of the increase in profits derived from the Group's international banking and investment banking businesses rather than from branch banking. Within UKBB, the increase in profits was attributable to a decrease in bad debt provisions.

Operating income actually declined slightly (to £3.45 billion from £3.47 billion the year before) and had been flat or falling for some time. Advances (lending) had fallen to £81.7 billion from £85.7 billion.

What is more, the Bank was facing heightened competition from other banks and building societies (thrifts) and from new competitors such as Marks and Spencer (a department store selling everything from ladies' underwear to frozen dinners and, now, financial services) and General Motors (which was heavily advertising its new credit card). Given this, and given the state of the British economy, an increase in operating income was unlikely in the foreseeable future. Therefore, redoubled efforts to squeeze costs were necessary to improve the cost-income ratio, which is studied carefully by shareholders and City analysts. Without further— admittedly painful—cost cutting, the cost-income ratio would rise, the share price would drop, and the Bank would be taken over as one competitor recently had been.

It took Tom twenty-five minutes to get through this material. He got tangled up in some of the math and had to take time to explain what concepts like *operating income* and *cost-income ratio* meant. That left a few minutes for questions. A woman in the front row, Sally, raised her hand and waved it back and forth. There was a collective groan among the people I was sitting near, and Tom pretended not to see her hand as he asked if there were any questions. After enduring a minute of this teasing, Sally stood up and said that she wanted to say a few words on behalf of the Staff Association. The Staff Association is one of two competing unions— the other being the Banking, Insurance, and Finance Union (BIFU)— that have organized employees in the Bank. Fewer than 25 percent of staff belong to either the Staff Association or BIFU, but both enter into collective bargaining with the Bank over contracts that cover all clerical staff.

"This is not a membership pitch," Sally said several times, "but, if more of us belonged to the Staff Association, we would have a greater chance of influencing things." Sarcastic comments from Tom ("But it's not a membership pitch!") and jeering from her colleagues grew each time she insisted that she was not canvassing for members, but the room quieted quickly when she moved on to describe the Staff Association's response to the Bank's results. "The Staff Association wants these profits to be reinvested in the people," she said. "Many parts of the Bank are operating short-staffed, many of us have not received the raises and promotions we have earned, and it isn't fair." Glaring at Tom, she said accusingly: "The Securities Centre is a perfect example. We need money for more staff, we need more PCs, we need to improve TecSec [the definitively imperfect computer software used to track the progress of security perfection], we need more training so that we can learn new jobs, too

many people have been stuck in the same job too long." Grumbles of assent were audible from the audience.

Looking chastened, Tom stammered that he agreed with her. More
money did need to be invested in the people, he said. Staffing and technology were a problem, not only in the Securities Centre, but in all parts
of the Bank. Tom complimented the group on all that they had done to
keep the place running despite those shortfalls. But, he said, the reality
was that the Bank was focused on cost cutting now. There was nothing
that he could do about that. He consented, however, to read the statement
from the Staff Association to the 10:30 group and to let Sally distribute
copies of it.

Standing in the back, Liz, one of the assistant managers, said that she
had a question: "What is the performance-related pay pot going to be?"
The size of the pool of money to be distributed to managers and employees as performance-related bonuses depends on the Bank's overall
profitability. Tom said that he had wondered about that figure too since
it should have been sent down with the results. It was not. "You know the
Bank," he said, rolling his eyes and laughing. Cutler, my doer 2 mentor,
leaned over to me and whispered that the Christmas bonus had been cut
to one-quarter of 1 percent of salary (less than £25 in Cutler's case) because of the new performance-related pay (PRP) scheme, so he was pretty
curious too about the size of the pot. "Not that it's likely to be much," he
frowned. "They're probably holding the numbers back because they're
embarrassed at how small they are." Someone within earshot chuckled in
solidarity. On the other side of the room, Liz continued to complain that
it was not right that the numbers had not been released. "I just read what
they send me," Tom said defensively. He agreed to call right away to find
out why the PRP figures had not been sent out yet.

Our group filed out as the 10:30 group showed up at the door. Jokes
were exchanged, and, as we walked up the stairs, I asked Cutler whether
he was surprised that the results were presented as bad news even though
they seemed so good. "No," he said. Overhearing us, Max—another
doer 2—said to me: "You're studying the culture, right? That's the culture. Everything is bad news. Otherwise, they'd have to pay us more." His
comment provoked a few laughs. "Still," Cutler said, "I don't suppose it's
worse here than anywhere else." Max nodded in agreement, and we all
went back to work.

Complaint and Complaisance

Financial results have great cultural significance in the Bank. That may
seem obvious: it is perhaps to be expected that a financial institution

would institutionalize financial concern in its members. Actually, however, a common complaint in the Bank is that management and staff are too insulated from financial results. As one disapproving manager put it: "They don't feel the pain." My observations tend to support this view; the financial performance of the Bank caused little pain that I could see. Nevertheless, financial results are an important justification for much of the negativity expressed toward the Bank. The following comment by an assistant manager is typical: "How do I know [that the culture needs to be changed]? Look around. Look at the results. Not the profit figure—that's meaningless. Look more closely. We aren't growing our lending book. Our costs are still too high. New competitors are out there, waiting to eat our lunch. We need to change." Invoking the Bank's poor results is an acceptable way of legitimating a wide variety of criticisms and complaints.

What is more, poor financial results are an important justification for many decisions made in the Bank, especially unpopular decisions involving cost cutting. As it was explained to me, employees were thought to be less likely to make the sacrifices necessary to cut costs if the financial results did not appear to mandate them. It was important, therefore, that the results and the surrounding publicity not have an adverse effect on these efforts. Attributing decisions, such as those to staff branches with fewer people or to cut year-end bonuses, to objective necessity created by short-termist "City analysts" or emergent "globalization" allows the exercise of power to be *euphemized* (see Bourdieu 1990, 126). It allows such decisions to be described as if they are not decisions at all, as if no decisionmaking is involved, but, rather, the poor results of the Bank speak for themselves (and what they say is: "Cut costs"). In other words, this euphemization of power allows all parties to deny conflicts of interests and purposefully misrecognize the locus of control in their relationship. It softens the exercise of control, makes it more gentle, but it also makes it less questionable and deflects responsibility for it away from management. The analysts or globalization are to blame, but there is no point blaming them, and, more important, there is no point blaming Bank management, who are only doing what they must.

For this sort of euphemization to work, the results have to be bad. Yet, as we have seen, the Bank's results during the period of study were equivocal. The results therefore have to be *dysphemized* in order for them to euphemize the exercise of power. Like euphemism, dysphemism is a ritual of politeness. If euphemism is the use of a mild, comforting, or evasive expression in place of one that is taboo, negative, offensive, or too direct, dysphemism is "the use of a negative or disparaging expression to describe something or someone, such as calling a Rolls-Royce a jalopy" or a carefully prepared meal something just thrown together (McArthur

1992, 328, 387). Or it is representing an 83 percent jump in profits to £767 million for the first six months of the year as bad news. Dysphemization is not deceit. The official truth about the Bank's results was not a fabrication. Operating income *was* flat; the cost-income ratio *was* higher than that of competitors. Rather, it was a legitimate, factual interpretation of an equivocal reality. In other cultural contexts, and with other ends in mind, other interpretations of the results would also have been possible.

The existence of such alternative ("piggy banks") interpretations was well-known at all levels of the Bank. Tabloids like the *Daily Mirror* are more widely read by staff in the Bank than is the *Financial Times*. News of BritArm's profits was widely reported on British radio and television and in all the national newspapers. Few reports went into detail about the difference between Group profits and UKBB profits. Few considered what the cost-income ratio or the operating income figure might reveal. By all accounts, most Bank staff found reinforcement—from family, friends, and customers—for the interpretation that BritArm was making embarrassingly fat profits. Most found this interpretation intuitively appealing. Still, almost all the employees to whom I spoke also expressed at least a grudging acceptance of the Bank's official, and more dismal, interpretation. Few found it as intuitive as the fat profits story (but then nobody expected it to be intuitive: after all, careful speaking notes were prepared to guide managers delivering a complex argument). Many found its precision and subtle accuracy appealing.

This may go some way toward explaining why financial results play such an important symbolic role in the Bank and yet cause no feelings of pain. The dichotomy reflects the power and also the limitations of what Berger and Luckmann (1967, 130) call *secondary socialization*. We may talk of organizations as being cultures whose members are socialized into its norms, values, and beliefs and come to define themselves, at least in part, as members of the organization. But we may do so only if we remember that they have been socialized before. As children, they internalized as objective reality the norms, values, and beliefs of society—more specifically, of that part of society into which they were born—and they formed their identity as members of that (part of) society. This is primary socialization: the childhood process through which an individual becomes a member of society. Secondary socialization is a subsequent process that inducts an already-socialized individual into a new sector of society—such as the Bank. Secondary socialization is seldom as powerful as primary socialization—except in cases where it is consistent with the already-formed self and the already-internalized world of primary socialization. The definitions of situations with which it provides members must compete with the definitions already provided by that outside world. The first time we learn something, we learn it as truth; the second time, we learn it as opinion. Largely because it is the only work culture known by employees (few of whom have worked elsewhere and few of whom look forward to working elsewhere), the Bank's culture is nevertheless potent—especially where it is consistent with that wider world and self.

The point is that it does us no good to treat the Bank as if it were an isolated society, cut off from the rest of the world. It is impossible to understand culture in BritArm without referring to the broader British culture—and the narrower occupational, class, and regional subcultures within it—in which the Bank is set and that, to some extent, it reflects. As its name suggests, being British is a defining (although not a determining) characteristic of BritArm. And, at the end of the day, people go home from the Bank. The meanings and definitions provided by the Bank must be able to survive the night in this broader cultural context.

In the case of the financial results, the interpretation consistent with primary socialization (the Bank is in almost too good financial shape) diverges from the interpretation mandated by secondary socialization (the Bank is in troubled financial shape). This conflict creates the potential for cynicism either about the interests behind the Bank's interpretation or about the media and its bias against banks. Both sorts of cynicism can to some degree be found in the Bank. However, the Bank's culture provides a legitimate way for both interpretations to coexist. It is only natural, I was told, that the Bank would have a different interpretation of events than would the man on the street. Bank staff in this situation "feel" the Bank to be doing fine even as they "know" that it is not. The primary interpretation is internalized at the same time as a secondary, contradictory interpretation is also understood—albeit in a different key (Goffman 1974, 45). The inconsistency is suspended by the cultural provision, not only of the uniform of the Bank's official ideology, but also of the skin of a way to derogate it: "That's the culture. Everything is bad news. Otherwise, they'd have to pay us more." By being able to complain about the culture in this innocuous way, the employees of BritArm are able to play along with the euphemization of power while displaying that they are wise to the disguise.

Connoting Culture

It is worth asking to what extent my presence prompted the comment: "That's the culture. Everything is bad news. Otherwise, they'd have to pay us more." It was prefaced with, "You're studying the culture, right?" which indicates that it was said for my benefit and that culture came into it because Max knew of my interest in learning about the culture. This is undeniable and presents complications for the study of lay ethnography. However, that Max's colleagues responded with laughter, and that it was a colleague and not I who replied to him, suggests that I was not the only—or even the most important—audience for his derogation. Also, one advantage of participant-observation over private interviews for the present study is that comments like these, even when made to me, were made in public. This means that it is likely that they reflect shared understandings (or shared pretenses). Informants had to talk to me in a way consistent with the way in which they talked to each other. Thus, even if Max's comment was for my sake phrased as being about *culture*, we can have confidence that its content expressed shared understandings.

It was widely known that I was at the Bank to study the culture, and, unprompted, people would regularly describe the culture to me. I make no inferences from that about how often the word *culture* itself was used in the Bank when I was not around. I *overheard* comments about the culture as well, and, certainly, it was the case that, without my needing to define or explain what *culture* meant, people at all levels of the Bank had descriptions of it ready to hand. Hearing these descriptions, what I came to learn was that people talked about *the Bank* in the same way that they talked about *the culture*. *The Bank* denotes the whole fifty thousand employees, £160 billion in assets, and extensive codified policies and procedures of BritArm UK. It also stands for various parts of that whole: most commonly, those parts diametrically opposed to the salient context of the speaker. So, for example, in branches, *the Bank* likely means the Head Office; in a given region, the other regions; and, among executives, regional, area, branch, lending, and administrative managers. But *the Bank* connotes not so much a group or an organization as a pattern of how things are done in (other parts of) BritArm UK. When talking among themselves, employees referred to *the Bank* more frequently than they did *the culture*, and most of what I record as lay ethnography in what follows comes from commentary that I heard or overheard about *the Bank* in its cultural connotation.

Consider the following examples to see how the two terms work together. "Our problem is our culture," explained Robert Christopher, human resources director. "We have good people, but after a while they tend to get sucked into the BritArm mind-set." "Christ," said one manager, apparently taking a sarcastic comment by me as evidence that I had gone native before my seventh month of fieldwork. "It usually takes years for the Bank to break people and make them so cynical and negative." "It's the culture," explained the assistant manager of a back office facility about another futile meeting to get his team leaders to focus less on following the rules and more on serving the branches. "It's the culture of the place," explained a middle manager about the thick stack of internal memos, action sheet addenda,[2] and other paperwork that he is sent every morning. "The Bank drowns you in paper." "You have to expect that in the Bank," explained a branch manager about the open laughter and guffaws from his staff that greeted the latest in CEO Michael Cole's series of videos, *Progressing the Vision*. "And you have to admit, it was pretty funny." "It's our culture," explains a senior clerk about one of the seemingly daily negative reports about BritArm in the British press. "We are terrible at PR." Indeed.

In the Communication Meeting presenting the half-year results, we see an example of how expressions of negativity about the Bank are typically used. Responding to a question about why the bonus figures had not been released with the profit figures, Tom says, with a rolling of the eyes and a laugh, "You know the Bank." *The Bank* here refers to the way in which the Head Office operates, and the derogation, its content left implicit, assumes that the negative views about this are so well-known by the audience that they need not be specified. It is an attempt to bring people together by invoking not just a common enemy but a shared understanding of that enemy. Tom is not wholly successful in this attempt. He is forced by Liz repeating her deprecation to maintain his role as manager, as the Bank's representative in that meeting. The audience does not allow him to become one of them, complaining right alongside them. Put on the defensive, he weakly shifts the blame ("I just read what they send me") and promises to look into the matter. Cultural competence and personal standing are required to use the tactics of negative lay ethnography successfully. Widely considered a poor manager within the Securities Centre, Tom succeeds more in affirming his reputation for being useless than in strengthening group bonds.

Complaining to Tom about the bonus figures not being released or about the need for more staff, better technology, and further training is not going to produce results. Officially, Tom is the appropriate person to whom to direct such complaints, but there is broad agreement with him when he says that there is nothing he can do about it. The official alternative channel of complaint is the Staff Association. But the teasing that Sally takes when she stands up to give the Staff Association's response to the results illustrates the lack of appetite for, and discomfort with, conflict

---

2. *Action sheet* is the name given in the Bank to any of the hundreds of pages of standard operating procedure documentation current in the organization. Collected in loose-leaf binders by every branch and office in the Bank, the action sheets are updated regularly.

and collective action. In part, this reflects a lack of faith that, even with the employees' support, the Staff Association would be able to solve their problems. But it also reflects the fact that behind the commonly heard complaints, which Sally accurately summarizes, there is an acquiescence to the status quo, an acceptance that costs do need to be cut, that delays in improvements to the technology are inevitable, and so on, even if that necessity and that inevitability do not feel right. The complaints provide some wriggle room to allow individuals and the group as a whole to find a comfortable position as they accommodate themselves to the imposed definition of their situation. That they would genuinely prefer those complaints to be redressed is clear from their grumbles of assent when Sally raised them. But to take them as *requests* for that redress or as indications of a readiness for action is to misread the culture as badly as Sally did when she was too obviously putting in a pitch for new members and, thus, got teased.

Pushing Paper

The results announcement was described from the vantage point of a Securities Centre. Less than a year old at that time, this particular Centre was one of sixteen such offices established around England as part of the Bank's cost-cutting drive, the aim in this case being to remove back office processes, such as the perfection of security, from branches and centralize them in specialist units. These units, it was explained to me, were to be run self-consciously as paper factories. The jobs were to be deskilled through subdivision, routinization, and, where possible, automation. Securities work had been a task performed by the most senior clerical staff as a necessary step in their career path to management. Typically, a securities clerk would have had more than five years' experience performing the more junior clerical tasks of processing checks, waiting on customers as a cashier (i.e., what in the United States would be called a *teller*) or at the Customer Service Desk, handling the paperwork associated with account openings and closings, and so on. Often tedious, securities work had the advantages of being technically challenging, providing professional contact with the lending manager and his or her assistant, and teaching the budding manager-to-be the ins and outs of securing loans.

This changed with the establishment of Securities Centres. Necessitated by the interpretation of the Bank's results as poor, the cost-cutting measures have been shaped by assumptions that ground the unpopular culture. One of the assumptions shaping the decision to cut costs by creating Securities Centres was articulated to me by one of BritArm UK's directors:

You have to understand that BritArm UK does not attract top-notch people. We do not attract people of the caliber, for example, of an investment bank. The people we attract are steady, able performers who desire security and direction. This is a generalization, of course, but it is broadly true, and we do ourselves no favors by pretending it isn't. Many of the people in this Bank really do want just to move paper from the left side of their desk to the right all day. Those are the people being put in places like the Securities Centres. And they are better off there.

This executive, recruited to BritArm from outside the Bank, still considers himself an outsider to the BritArm culture and is more outspoken than most BritArm directors. The sentiments that he expresses were, however, echoed across the Bank, albeit less forthrightly. "Horses for courses" was the cliché most often used. Find the paper pushers, and create places like the Securities Centres to allow them to push paper exclusively. Find the salesmen, and put them in front of the customer. Find the leaders, and groom them for top jobs. Recognize that most Bank hires are incapable of performing in multiple roles, and subdivide the work accordingly.

Not surprisingly, the Securities Centres are not popular. Lending managers complain of delays and a loss of control over the process. That is, they miss having the securities clerks work directly for them and being able to look over their shoulders and direct their priorities. Employees fear that assignment to a Securities Centre is a stigma and will hurt their careers. The technology designed to partially deskill the job has deskilled it less than expected, so more senior people are required than were budgeted for, leading to cost overruns. A hiring freeze in the Bank and difficulty moving staff from branches to the Securities Centres have led to a shortage of staff at the junior levels of doer 1 and doer 2. Doubts about the technology and about the ability of very junior people to handle security work have led to a perceived need for the assistant manager to check all the work of the doers. Delays have resulted. The assistant managers complain that they are checkers, not managers, and that the job is not interesting.

In sum, the staff of the Securities Centres have a lot to complain about. But, under almost constant criticism from other parts of the Bank, especially lending managers, about the service that they provide, they also find themselves in the position of defending, not only themselves individually, but also the very idea of Securities Centres—that the job can be done more efficiently if partially centralized and partially automated. They have come, in other words, to identify with the Securities Centres, and they take pride in the reports from the Bank's internal auditors that praise the reliability of their finished product as being higher than it was when the job was done in branches (apparently having control of the process had for lending managers meant the ability to cut corners). This explains some of the reluctance to pursue their various complaints and publicly seek redress. They feel defensive when they hear outsiders making the same criticisms that they make themselves about the tedium of the work, the inadequacy of the technology, or the abilities of some of the staff. Thus, the same love-hate relationship that we see between employees and the Bank as a whole—and the same desire to defend with one audience what is deprecated with another—operates within the Securities Centres as well.

So, although at one level it is true to say that the Bank (or the Securities Centre) does not think much of its staff and that, in return, its staff do not think much of it, at another level it is patently false. There is tremendous loyalty to and affection for the organization among its employees. Indeed, the Bank as a whole is described as offering something akin to a British version of the American Dream. I heard from manager after grateful manager that the Bank had taken him (most managers *were* men) far from his lowly beginnings and limited educational attainments to unexpected social standing and opportunity. Far, that is, from the mediocre prospects that he—or others attracted to the Bank—could have expected.

The Bank fosters lasting friendships and many marriages. It has Culture, with a capital *C,* in a big way: ritual and myth; artifacts and idols. Yet, as these managers compare the Bank to the models held up as exemplary organizational cultures in the press and in British popular culture more widely, they find in their culture the antithesis of the ideal and, therefore, much to self-deprecate.[3] They justify their organizational loyalty to themselves by telling themselves that, at least within the universe of organizations that are likely to hire people like them, things are no worse in BritArm than anywhere else.

In the Field

The vignette of the results announcement highlights and illustrates some of the key themes of the unpopular culture in BritArm that will be analyzed in more detail in the coming chapters: the uses of complaint about the Bank, such as bonding, blaming, self-positioning, and euphemizing

---

3. Fowler (1965) noted that, as early as 1926, "deprecate (do the reverse of pray for) often appears in print, whether by the writer's or the compositor's blunder, in place of depreciate (do the reverse of praise)." By now, *self-deprecate* has come to mean "self-deprecate" and is the more commonly used of the two reflexive forms. The distinction between *deprecate* and *derogate/ depreciate* (both of which mean "to belittle") is important, however, and discussed in chapter 4.

power; the way in which complaints must be misrecognized if they are to be effective in those uses; the cultural competence required for this; the fact that the resulting pattern of complaint is best seen, not as opposing the culture that it critiques, but, rather, as revealing its assumptions and reproducing them. More generally, what I hope this vignette shows is the subtlety involved: the expressions of negativity cannot be dismissed as superficial, but neither can they be taken at face value. Just as BritArm UK cannot be understood without reference to the broader society of which it is part, the negative lay ethnography cannot be understood outside the context in which it is produced. Questions of how it operates, the impact it has, and the ways in which it is patterned can be answered only with what Geertz (1973b, 7) calls *thick description*. It is necessary to locate this negative lay ethnography in the ongoing improvisation and strategizing of Bank employees as they strive to do their jobs, advance their careers, enjoy themselves, and make sense of what is going on around them.

Fieldwork is the appropriate method for this task, and *ethnography* is the name given to the resulting thick description of BritArm UK. The realist ethnography (Van Maanen 1988) that forms the bulk of the study is based on eight months of full-time fieldwork performed over a twelve-month period during 1994 and 1995 in the British Armstrong Bank in England and follow-up interviews of managers and employees as well as three short periods of observation in the six years following.

My fieldwork was largely financed by sponsorship fees paid by BritArm to a Massachusetts Institute of Technology (MIT) project called the Delta Project (the results of which can be found in Hax and Wilde [1999]). The work with BritArm started as a small pilot study investigating the different leadership styles of two managers in the Bank who were deemed by its chairman to be successful in different ways. This resulted in my going to England to spend two weeks with Edward Tollerton—one of the Bank's regional executive directors—and his team and an MIT colleague going to the Bank's U.S. subsidiary to spend time with a manager there. The Bank's representatives on the project were sufficiently impressed with this early work that they were persuaded to allow me to spend an extended period of time observing and even working in various parts of the U.S. and U.K. banks, shadowing managers, and conducting interviews. The idea of the study was that I would return from the field with some ideas for the Bank about how the U.S. and U.K. operations could learn from each other. With the sale, however, of the U.S. bank halfway through my time there, interest in this topic waned, and I returned to the United Kingdom and was given latitude in choosing for myself a focus of study.

The research design took the shape of a T, with the vertical stem representing a long period of study in a single part of BritArm and the horizontal stem representing a series of shorter periods studying other parts of the Bank. I would stay in one place long enough to understand it in depth and to learn enough about the Bank's culture to be able to make better sense of my broader (and, necessarily, shallower) observations of the rest of the organization. Conversely, my experience traveling widely in the Bank would, by helping me understand the variety of its subcultures, reveal the limits, and possibilities, of generalizing from one part to the whole. The locations and schedules in England were arranged with the help of Tollerton. It was he who suggested that my long stay be with the Securities Centre. This choice resulted from his unexpected assent to my slightly cynical request that he allow me to spend time in the unit having the most trouble at the moment. In my previous fortnight in his region, I had heard only good things about his leadership, and, in my interviews, the region had been so often compared favorably to some other regions of the Bank that I was suspicious that his selection of interview candidates had been calculated to give me a certain impression. These suspicions proved to have been groundless, and the Securities Centre offered an excellent base for the study both because of the friendly, welcoming attitude of the management and staff there and because of that Centre being in the midst of a self-described crisis, which meant that certain assumptions that might otherwise have been completely taken for granted were more open to recognition and question.

After spending three months at the Securities Centre and very nearly, I am told, attaining the proficiency to be entrusted with some aspects of doer 2 work, I left to spend two weeks shadowing a chief manager, two weeks each in three branches of different sizes (large, medium, and small—each of which is said in the Bank to have a different feel to it), a week each in another Securities Centre and in three other back office units, a week in another branch, and a week in Regional Office. With the exception of the second Securities Centre, all this time was spent in Tollerton's region. I also spent a scattered five days at the Bank's Staff College attending a course and a number of end-of-course dinners where I had the opportunity to meet managers and staff from other regions. I spent three days with managers from one of these regions, including my one and only intervention effort in the Bank: an abysmal one-day workshop on communication and learning that I led that revealed more about what I still had to learn about the Bank's culture than it did about what the participants had to learn about communication and learning. I spent three weeks in various parts of Head Office in London and, finally, after six months back in the United States, made a week-long visit to attend

Tollerton's retirement party and to meet again with many of my informants. During the long process of creating an ethnography from my field
notes, I have kept in close touch with Tollerton, been back to BritArm on
three occasions for short periods of observation (three days once, two
days twice), and have conducted twenty-eight additional interviews with
old informants and with BritArm managers who have attended INSEAD
(the European Institute of Business Administration) executive programs.

During the period of fieldwork, I attended many private dinner parties, many pub lunches,[4] one beer breakfast, and every Bank party I could
get myself invited to. In the early stages of the fieldwork, I tried taking
notes while in the Bank but found that this attracted too much attention,
and often suspicion, except in formal interview situations. Outside interviews, therefore, I kept a small notebook in my coat pocket and jotted
down what reminders I could to be fleshed out that evening either on my
laptop or into a Dictaphone on my commute home. In addition, as inse-
cure field-workers are wont to do, I collected all manner of paperwork.
There was no brochure or report too insignificant to escape my collection
(although there were many that proved too sensitive for me to be allowed
to take away). By the end, I had accumulated a large filing cupboard full
of such materials.

The word *informant* is an unfortunate one for the people I came to know
in the Bank. They became my friends. The fear of the ethnographer is
that, with the publication of the manuscript, he moves from being a
friend to being a betrayer of confidence. That this book, with its emphasis on the unpopular aspects of the Bank and its blunt description so uncharacteristic of the tact adhered to in the Bank, will be seen by some as
a betrayal is very likely. That I felt the need to withhold additional, richer
examples of many of the phenomena that I describe here to preserve the
anonymity and save the feelings of people I came to care about is a fact.
The advantage of ethnography as a method is that it forces us to shed the
metaphoric white lab coat and live among the people we are studying.
Ethnography offers insights unattainable by other means. But that white
coat, and the claims of objectivity and distance that it represents, is the
armor of the social scientist. Without it, we researchers are implicated in
our research. We must bear responsibility for our findings, our creation.

These dilemmas confront the lay ethnographers of the firm even more
acutely, of course. For them, audience, subject, and informants are one
and the same, and this has markedly censorial effects on what gets said

---

4. I found these such a useful, and admittedly pleasurable, source of information that I made
a bit of an embarrassing name for myself in the Securities Centre by often taking both first and
second lunch—different staff go at different times to make sure the phones are always manned.

about the culture and how. Before we can examine these lay ethnographic effects in BritArm, we first need to set some context for that discussion. Specifically, we need to understand what sense culture makes in the organization—what concepts of culture inform the lay ethnography that we find there—and why talking about the organization in cultural terms has proved to be so influential. This is the task of the next chapter.

3

orgɑnizɑtionɑl culture

Has the word *culture* acquired the same
cultural status as a cough?
—Christopher Clausen

Organizational culture is popular. The fact that members of organizations regularly ruminate on their cultures, pass judgments on them, and place weight on these judgments—whatever the verdict—is testimony to the degree to which the term *organizational culture* has established itself in the lexicon of corporate America and Britain. To understand why this is the case and what impact this has had on organizations in general, and on BritArm in particular, we need to understand how this idea of culture is thought of and how it is used.

Defining *culture* is not a simple task. *Culture* is notoriously polysemic. Berger (1995, 3) notes that this is in part because it is the common property of a variety of users who employ it to different purposes. Moreover, not only does *culture* mean different things to different people, but it also means different things to the same people. There is a distinction—although blurred, as all these distinctions are—for example, between what we might call the *aesthetic* sense of *culture,* culture as intellectual and artistic expression, and the *anthropological* sense of *culture,* culture as a distinct way of life. However, within anthropology alone there are over 250 different definitions of *culture:* Kroeber and Kluckhohn (1952) famously catalog 164, and Keesing's (1974) review adds 86 more without being complete.

With all these definitions to choose from, not to mention numerous sociological ones, management scholars have chosen to invent scores of their own. As Van Maanen (1984, 216) quips: "Those of us who are the culture vultures of organization studies are a fairly contentious lot and do not frequently adopt one another's definitions." Authors writing for a practitioner audience have, in turn, mixed, matched, and sometimes

mangled these scholarly definitions of culture in organizations, occasionally even leaving the exercise to the reader. Neuhauser, Bender, and Stromberg (2000, 4) provide an excellent example of this in their book about
how to create organizational cultures for the Internet Age, *Culture.com*.
They begin by listing several definitions of *culture* and then say: "All of
these definitions are accurate and work well as a base for reading this
book. Pick the definition that makes the most sense to you or fits best with
the way people in your company would say it."

This do-it-yourself approach to the definition of *culture* seems to con-
firm the worst fears of scholars such as Schein (1991, 243), who has argued
that the concept of *culture* in organizations cannot be useful if "we cannot
agree on how to define it, 'measure' it, study it, and apply it in the real
world of organizations." The differences between the various definitions
of *culture* are not (always) merely cosmetic. There are deep disagreements,
for example, about whether culture resides in material artifacts and publicly meaningful forms that can be seen and heard or in people's ideas and
interpretations of those artifacts. That is, does culture exist in people's
heads or somewhere else? There are disagreements about whether culture is by definition something that is shared or whether, as Martin (1992,
152) claims, the "absence of consensus does not indicate an absence of
culture, but rather the presence of a fragmented culture."

In other words, do all organizations (indeed, all groups, however
bounded) have cultures, or do only those that are sufficiently homogeneous in their values—or assumptions, or artifacts, or whatever else we
may decide that culture may consist of? Indeed, the diversity among the
many scholarly definitions of *organizational culture* is such that, if we try to
isolate what is common to all of them, we end up with not much at all: a
vague and shapeless resemblance to what Young (1991, 91) memorably
calls "that vacuous 'way things are done around here.'" The result is that
basic questions—for example, What is organizational culture? Where
does it reside? How can we know an organization's culture? Can culture
change be managed? If so, how do we know what changes to make?—
continue to defy scholarly consensus.

Does this matter? It doesn't seem to matter in the American or British
business press, where questions such as these are conveniently ignored,
their answers taken for granted and left implicit. Thus, the *Economist*
can state without embarrassment or elaboration: "The harsh impact of
downsizing on things like morale and corporate culture is well known"
("Unthinking Shrinking" 1995). Really? Well-known to whom? To the ed-
itors of the *Wall Street Journal*, apparently, who printed a front-page story
that noted matter-of-factly that the "downside of downsizing" is that
"risk-taking dwindles because the culture of cost-cutting emphasizes the

certainties of cutting costs over the uncertainties—and expense—of trying something new" ("Some Companies Cut Costs" 1995). Facile assumptions by journalists about the transparency of culture, and asinine
statements about cultures of cost cutting that emphasize cutting costs, irritate us business school academics, who feel possessive of the concept of
organizational culture (as our assumptions about culture, in turn, irritate anthropologists [Jordon 1989, 2]). Statements like these seem to make pre-
scient Allaire and Firsirotu's (1984, 194) concern that, as the proposition
that organizations have cultural properties gained in popularity, it might
lose rigor and be reduced to "an empty, if entertaining, catch-all con-
struct explaining everything and nothing."

Perhaps this is to see it backward, however. Perhaps it is not so much
that, as the idea of organizational culture became popular, it was emptied
of concrete meaning as it is that it has remained popular precisely *because*
it is vague and suggestive and has become more so over time. The idea
of organizational culture rose to prominence with *In Search of Excellence*
(Peters and Waterman 1982)—at a time when economic weakness and
the success of Japanese multinationals had Americans and Britons alike
wondering about the cultural determinants of success. But this does not
explain its longevity—why the idea did not come and go as other management fads (and, for that matter, the fortunes of many Japanese multinationals) have done. The continued steady stream of new self-help
guides to organizational culture, and newly revised versions of old ones,
does not explain its longevity either: none of these books has had the impact of *In Search of Excellence,* and, anyway, they are more the product of
the continued corporate interest in culture than its cause.

I would argue that the fecundity and longevity of the idea of organizational culture is specifically related to the fact that the dominant notion
of organizational culture in popular usage is the lowest-common-
denominator one—a vague, suggestive fuzz. Alvesson (1993, 3) calls *organizational culture* "a word for the lazy," although he does not mean this as a
compliment. The word is economical: it connotes a broad range of in-
tangible somethings or other. It also has high face validity: we all think
that we know what it means, that what it means goes without saying.
These qualities may not make for clarity or precision of meaning, but
whenever have clarity and precision been the determining factors of
word choice, especially in corporate settings (see Jackall 1988, 161)? The
fuzziness and ambiguity of *organizational culture,* the fact that consensus
about its meaning is not required for its use, are not incidental; these
things are precisely what makes culture so attractive to talk about. Culture has become a legitimate way in which to cover up uncertainty of
mind and paper over differences of opinion. As Berger (1995, 14) says:

"Efforts to be precise in ordinary language-use risk bringing routine social interaction to a sudden halt." Asking people to be clear about what
they mean when they use the word *culture* is as rude as asking what they
mean when they way "Fine" in response to "How are you?" Had they
wanted to be more specific, they would have used a word other than *culture*. Culture may be less like a cough and more like a yawn: contagious
and with the effect of putting the mind a little bit to sleep. In such circumstances, one need not be a disciple of Wittgenstein to see that, to understand the meaning of the word *culture*, we must look at how it is used,
not at how it may be defined abstractly.

Usage in the Business Press

If the idea of organizational culture was born in academic studies of the
sociology of organizations and introduced to the popular culture of
America and Britain by management self-help books, it is the day-to-day
messages of the business press that have done the most to institutionalize
the notion that culture is a normal part of organizations. It is with the
business press, then, that we should begin the investigation of the idea's
use. What follows is a review of the references to organizational culture
and corporate culture in the pages of the *Wall Street Journal* and the *Economist* during the period of my study of BritArm: January 1994–August
2001. I have chosen these newspapers because of their wide circulation
(the former in the United States, the latter in the United Kingdom, although both are available in both countries), their influence on managers
and other decisionmakers, and their editorial conservatism. More to the
point, I have chosen them because I read them regularly. The review that
I have undertaken would have been immensely difficult using a database
search tool such as Lexis-Nexis or ABI/Inform. Almost without exception, every issue of these two newspapers contains some reference to culture. An ABI/Inform search for articles containing the word *culture* during that time period turns up an average of 6.9 articles in each issue of the
Wall Street Journal and 6.5 in each issue of the *Economist*, for a total of
18,953 articles in all.

Many of these articles do not refer specifically to *organizational culture*
(or to *corporate culture* or *company culture* or *business culture*—except where
noted, I use these terms interchangeably, as do the two newspapers). Yet
separating out those that *are* about organizational culture is not straightforward. We cannot just search for terms like *organizational culture* or *corporate culture* since, when the organizational context is clear, the modifiers *organizational* and *corporate* are not used. Instead, it is necessary to read each
article to determine the nature of the reference to culture. If we estimate

that it takes five minutes to read each article in sufficient detail, then this is approximately a fifteen-hundred-hour task. By choosing two newspapers that I read and clip every week, I spread this time requirement over eight years, making such a review manageable.

In addition to filtering out articles that referred to nonorganizational forms of culture, I also ignored all articles that made only passing reference to organizational culture. This step was important because what I required for the content analysis was a sample of articles in which the concept of *organizational culture* was used with sufficient elaboration that the underlying assumptions about what *culture* means and how it operates could be deduced. I was left with 382 articles one of whose main themes was the culture of an organization.

I then created a high-level categorization scheme for the articles. I distinguished between four ways in which organizational culture is invoked in the two newspapers. These are as follows (with the number of articles in each category given in parentheses): the effects of culture on organizational performance (107); the effects of culture on organizational change (68); the effects of culture on organizational mergers, acquisitions, and alliances (92); and the relation between the national culture and the cultures of particular organizations (57). I subsequently checked each of these categories for two things. First, I made sure that all four were equally used by the two newspapers. They were, and, in general, the *Wall Street Journal* and the *Economist* use *organizational culture* in identical ways. Second, I made sure that all four were consistently represented across the entire time period. They were, and, in general, I found no discernible difference in the usage of *organizational culture* over the period 1994–2001. The meaning of the term seems to have been fixed by 1994 and to have remained unchanged since then. Through the entire time period, *culture* is not put in scare quotes, nor is it defined before it is used. Apparently, readers are assumed to understand what *culture* and associated terms such as *strong culture, culture clash,* and *cultural fit* mean. Indeed, by 1996, culture was so well established as a self-evident property of corporations that the *Wall Street Journal* could run the following front-page headline: "At ABB, Globalization Isn't Just a Buzzword: It's a Corporate Culture" ("At ABB" 1996). Once a trendy management buzzword itself, *corporate culture* is now the very antithesis. It is—since 1994, if not before—real, normal, obvious.

Next, I subdivided the articles within each category into various themes, which I describe below. I discuss each of the four first-level categories in turn to explain the theories in use that they suggest about how culture's influence on organizations is made manifest, the degree to which culture may be managed, how particular cultures may be known, the ways in which culture is thought to be shaped by the organization's environment, and what characterizes good and bad organizational culture. Roughly speaking, we can match these as follows: implicit in articles referring to the effects of culture on organizational performance are assumptions about how culture's influence is made manifest; implicit in articles about the effects of culture on organizational change are assumptions about the degree to which culture may be managed; implicit in articles making predictions about the effect of culture on proposed mergers and acquisitions are assumptions about how cultures can be known and accurately described; and implicit in articles about the relation between the national culture and the cultures of particular organizations are assumptions about how an organization's environment shapes its culture. Furthermore, implicit in articles of all four categories are assumptions about what sorts of organizational cultures are good and what sorts are bad.

GOOD AND BAD CULTURE

Common to virtually all the articles that mention organizational culture is a normative and instrumental attitude toward culture, an evaluative stance that judges the cultures under consideration in the light of whether they lead to positive outcomes for their respective organizations. The only exceptions to this rule are a few whimsical articles such as a profile of Paul Wolsfeld, a man who has ridden his bicycle around the world collecting corporate trivia that may—or, then again, may not—reveal important insights about the cultures of the companies he visits (BritArm, he notes, has among its archives a German bomb, with parachute attached, that landed without exploding outside the front entrance of the Bank's London Head Office during World War II: testimony, perhaps, to the importance that the Bank places on its British heritage) (see "A Modern Don Quixote" 1998). The rest of the references assess organizational cultures as being either good or bad. If culture is neutral, it seldom makes the news.

There is a clear pattern to which kinds of cultures are described favorably and which unfavorably. First of all, cultures that are good are those that match the demands of the organization's competitive environment. The *Wall Street Journal,* for example, attributes the success of Philip Morris over its rival RJR in the embattled tobacco business to the fact that RJR does not have the same sort of "cigarette culture" that Philip Morris does: "Most of the [RJR] executives don't smoke cigarettes. The glass ashtrays in the waiting area of RJR's small corporate office are often filled with miniature rolls of Life-Savers." The headquarters of Philip Morris, on the other hand, is one of the few buildings in New York exempt from local indoor air-quality laws; ashtray cans adorn every lobby, and the company has "a strong, stable reserve of managers with a singular passion for cigarettes." A former top industry executive is quoted as saying: "The tobacco business has gotten to the point now that you have to be a true believer to really make things happen, and the Philip Morris guys are true believers. They eat it, breathe it, sleep it, and make it. They don't accept the government's premise that they are evil. They have no hang-ups" ("Philip Morris's Passion" 1995).

The point is not just about passionate beliefs; it is about the fit between those beliefs and the competitive environment. It is possible to have the wrong sort of passionate beliefs. The *Economist* writes, for example, that "the freewheeling culture of the Internet could be on the way out" because, "in the wake of the dotcom meltdown, it has become clear that oft-repeated Internet shibboleths such as 'information wants to be free' may not make any business sense." It notes that almost all the dot-com companies that failed were those that were compatible with "the hippy culture that has infused the Internet" and that those that remain in business are introducing subscriptions and fees. "If it comes to a choice between profitability and the survival of the Internet's traditional culture, it is not hard to guess which will prevail" ("Off with Their Beards" 2001).

The implicit theory of what makes for a good organizational culture is not, however, a pure contingency model. Or at least it is a contingency model only in a weak sense. There are some cultural characteristics that are universally described as good or bad for organizations today and in the future. This does not rule out that these cultural characteristics may have been in times past, or may be in some sheltered contexts, less necessary or less dangerous, but there is a strong assumption in the American and British business press that forces such as competition and globalization imply that, eventually, all companies in all industries and even organizations such as nonprofits, unions, and governments face a similar set of conditions calling for a similar set of organizational cultural characteristics. The implicit theory thus becomes a contingency model without contingency.

In particular, a "bureaucratic culture" is always negative. By itself, this does not tell us much since, in ordinary usage, *bureaucracy*, like *culture*, is a vague term that stands for several things. Seldom used anymore in Weber's (1978, 956) sense—notwithstanding Perrow's (1986, 5) best efforts—*bureaucracy* has become a pejorative signifying "unnecessary complications, constraining standardization, [and] the stifling of individual personality" (Crozier 1964, 1). The phrase *bureaucratic culture* seems to take this dissociation to the next step, indicating an organization whose members think and act like stereotypical bureaucrats whether or not the rules, offices, record keeping, and other constituting characteristics of a bureaucracy are present. The stereotype is well enough understood that it can be invoked without elaboration. For example, in discussing the restructuring efforts of a number of German companies, the *Economist* notes: "A lot of companies have refused to take their full draught of medicine. Siemens has tried hard to cut costs but has yet to tackle a bureaucratic culture and plethora of under-performing businesses" ("Boom and Gloom" 1997). No more is said in the article about Siemens or its bureaucratic culture.

When it is elaborated on, bureaucratic culture is revealed to be characterized by four things: slow and centralized decisionmaking; insufficient attention paid to organizational performance; risk aversion; and inward focus. Thus, Lufthansa's efforts "to shake off any remaining bureaucratic vestiges from its days as a government-owned company" are described as "a big cultural change at a place once known for layers of management that slowed decision-making" ("Lufthansa Is Waking Up" 1997). The World Bank is said to be in the midst of a transformation from "a 'bureaucratic' culture into a 'results-oriented' one" ("World Bank's New Emphasis" 1997). Hewlett-Packard's new CEO is trying to change that company's once-vaunted culture—dubbed *the HP Way*—back to the way it used to be, as represented in mantras such as "No politics, no bureaucracy." The *Economist* reports that the HP Way "had become a recipe for inward focus and bureaucratic paralysis" and "an excuse for all sorts of bad habits, particularly slowness and risk-aversion" ("Rebuilding the Garage" 2000). And General Motors (like Hewlett-Packard, one of the original excellent companies, but one that lost its exemplary-culture status earlier and more thoroughly) is described as having a culture of bureaucracy and complacency, like all empires in their decline, one in which "meritocracy gives way to an introverted oligarchy that wastes its talents vying for position within the imperial court, rather than expanding the empire's borders" ("The Decline and Fall" 1998).

More common than bureaucratic cultures are cultures described as having only one of those four characteristics, and that is considered bad enough. By combining all four of them in the same organization, the bureaucratic culture represents the epitome of bad organizational culture. It is the anticulture. Indeed, bureaucracy is so far from the presumed ideal of organizational culture that practitioner-oriented writing about organizational culture sometimes portrays bureaucracy and culture as if these are two different modes of organizing (e.g., Ouchi 1981, 88–89).

What, then, are the cultural characteristics universally described as good? Naturally, they are the opposite of the bureaucratic ones. Most common are references to the ideal of an entrepreneurial, innovative, risk-accepting organizational culture. But organizations are more often described as falling short of this ideal than as meeting it. For example: "If CERN had had a thriving technology park around it, and had embraced an entrepreneurial culture that encouraged its young scientists to go out and commercialize their ideas, Europe as a whole might have profited more from the web" ("Cause for ConCERN?" 2000). Or: "The fault lies with the culture. The firm has stifled innovation and prevented new ideas from getting to market quickly. Years after P&G developed its tissue-towel products, they have only just started to be rolled out globally. 'We're slower than my great-grandma,' says one executive" ("Jager's Gamble" 1999).

Even when the organization has enjoyed financial success and its culture seems to be popular with members, that organizational culture still comes under question if it differs too greatly from this supposed ideal. For example: "Closely held, debt-free and notoriously risk-averse, Bertelsmann jealously guards a distinct corporate culture that was fostered by Mr. Mohn and is still manifest in the company's business dealings 15 years after he retired as its chairman. For years, Mr. Mohn's prudent philosophy served Bertelsmann well. A mandatory 15% rate of return on every project that it pursues has saved the company from risky business and costly mistakes. But in today's high-stakes entertainment industry, analysts warn that such wariness may equal weakness" ("Mogul Reinhard Mohn" 1997). It is not so much that entrepreneurial, innovative, and risk-accepting cultures are thought to be good because they are the sorts of cultures that successful organizations have; rather, the credibility of a firm's success—whether it is grounded on mere fortune or is justified, whether it is sustainable—is evaluated in part on the basis of how good the organization's culture is judged to be. To take another example, the *Economist* reports that, despite environmental disaster, cheap oil, and a stagnant home market, "Exxon is one of America's most successful companies." Noting that the corporation "is built on two pillars: conservative financial management and a conservative corporate culture," the *Economist* admits that this conservatism has led Exxon to avoid the mistakes of its major competitors, which had made risky and, ultimately, disappointing investments while Exxon had used its cash to buy back its own shares. "It worked," the newspaper says, "yet it also looks like a recipe for stagnation." Arguing that "the culture has its weak spots," the article concludes weakly that, in balance, perhaps its culture is not Exxon's biggest problem ("Inside the Empire" 1994).

Whereas the people in bureaucratic cultures are complacent about organizational performance or are too distracted by internal maneuvering and infighting to pay attention to it, the people in ideal cultures are focused on performance. Microsoft's success—as well as its problems with the Justice Department—for example, are attributed in part to its "super-aggressive culture personified by the founder, Bill Gates" ("Play Nicely" 1998). In its obituary for former Coca-Cola CEO Robert Goizueta, the

Wall Street Journal's Paul Gigot comments that Goizueta created more wealth, had a larger impact on the world, and generally "counted for more in the 1990s" than Bill Clinton. This was largely due, Gigot claims, to Goizueta's "seizing the global market and instilling a culture of competition" in Coke, a culture that allowed the company to generate large returns for its shareholders ("Bill Clinton?" 1997). Whatever *a culture of competition* may mean—Gigot does not say—it hardly seems to have outlived Goizueta: within four years of his death, Coke's profits had halved, and the company was being described as "a slow-moving, centralized bureaucracy, dangerously out of touch with local market trends" because of its "command and control culture" ("New Formula Coke" 2001).

It is an open question whether Coke had quickly shed its culture of competition and acquired a bureaucratic culture or whether, as the company's fortune's diminished, the *perception* of its culture changed. Given that organizational cultures are never as univalent as they are usually made out to be, it is possible to highlight different elements of them at different times and, thus, find a consistent link between culture and performance. Given assumptions about what sorts of organizational cultures lead to good performance and what sorts to bad, we may more easily recognize the competitive aspects of a high-performing organization and the bureaucratic aspects of a poor-performing one.

Finally, cultures that are cohesive or intimate are described as being good. The following front-page headline from the *Wall Street Journal* exemplifies this: "Lennar Thrives as Oddball Culture Helps to Tie Home Builder Together." The article describes how managers in Lennar are united by the requirement that they memorize poetry written by CEO Stuart Miller in the style of children's author Dr. Seuss and by their having been "inculcated with the company's mantra to maximize return on net assets" ("Lennar Thrives" 2001). That this ability of organizational cultures to bind groups with different interests is understood to be fragile can be seen in the fact that, much more than other positive cultural attributes, it is mentioned as being under threat. Reporting the ousting of Goldman Sachs's co–chief executive, Jon Corzine, for example, the *Economist* writes: "The danger is that the brusque treatment of Mr. Corzine, and a perception that Goldman's investment-banking side has scored a victory over its trading arm will unleash further conflict. That could make for a bumpy road to the IPO, and, by damaging Goldman's traditionally cohesive culture, reduce its chances of a successful long-term future" ("Palace Coup" 1999).

Similarly, considering Ikea's expansion into America, the *Economist* asks: "As the firm's operations became ever more global, could Ikea retain the intimate corporate culture that was an important part of its success?

In many ways, Ikea is still seeking answers" ("Furnishing the World" 1994). Percy Barnevik—for whose ABB *globalization* is, not just a buzz-word, but a corporate culture—is seen as ambitious for his decision "to expand globally during the 1990s even while trying to keep a cohesive identity and culture" ("A Great Leap" 2001). And Delta Airlines is de-scribed by the *Wall Street Journal* as having lost its "culture of the 'Delta family,'" a culture that prevailed before a large downsizing in 1997 ("How Delta's Pilots Mobilized" 2001). Economic downturns, internal growth, corporate politics—all these are thought to affect whether a culture can be cohesive.

Overall, then, we can infer a representative set of labels that are ap-plied to good and bad cultures from the way in which the business press talks about organizational culture:

Good	Bad
Not Bureaucratic	Bureaucratic
Entrepreneurial	Command and Control
Innovative	Risk Averse
Competitive	Complacent
Cohesive	Insular
Intimate	Formal
Scrappy	Staid

The list is not completely matched: there is no single label as compli-mentary as *bureaucratic* is derogatory. What is important to understand about these labels is that, although they facilitate the telling of a fairly co-herent story about good and bad organizational cultures, they get applied *after* judgment has been passed about goodness or badness. In part, this is because organizational cultures are always multifaceted and some facets may be considered good, others bad—as we saw above, Coca-Cola is likely accurately described both as competitive and as bureaucratic—whereas most facets are probably neither obviously good nor obviously bad. Organizational cultures are virtually never written about in neutral terms, however. Instead, articles tend to highlight those aspects of the cul-ture that fit the tone of the argument being made, eliding other aspects.

Equally important, however, is the fact that these labels are inherently value laden. It is not necessary to explain to readers that a bureaucratic culture is a negative thing. Indeed, explanation would be required if a re-porter wanted to claim that, in some special circumstance, a bureaucratic culture should be viewed positively. More likely, a different label would be used. When the *Wall Street Journal* wrote praising the culture of McDon-ald's, it considered the strict uniformity, rule following, and hierarchy to be, not bureaucratic, but "military" ("You're in the Army Now" 1995). When Pepsi's culture was described as being for far too long "exemplified by flashy ideas, big spending, and rapid management turnover," it was described, not as entrepreneurial, innovative, or risk taking, but, rather, as "flashy" and "out of control" ("Pepsi Challenge" 1997). When Rubbermaid faced high turnover among senior executives and poor relations with retailers, its culture was characterized as "high-pressure" and "numbers-driven," not as "competitive" or "superaggressive," as was successful Microsoft's ("Rubbermaid Tries to Regain" 1995; "Play Nicely" 1998).

We have seen that the particular organizations held up as examples in the organizational culture self-help manuals have changed over time but that the generic model of the exemplary culture has remained more or less constant. Here, we see the day-to-day rhetorical strategies that are used to insulate this model from empirical challenge as an unattainable ideal.

CULTURE'S EFFECTS

How is culture thought to have the effects on organizational behavior that are claimed for it? How is its impact on the organization made manifest? A good place to search for the answers to these questions is with the most concrete references to culture. For example, what does it mean that the nuclear operations of Ontario Hydro "lack a strong safety culture" other than that the company has a poor safety record ("Hydrophobia" 1997)? What does it mean that Kingston Technology has a "service culture" other than that it provides good customer service ("Doing the Right Thing" 1995)? What does it mean that "switching lay at the heart of the telephone industry's culture" other than that switches were a central technology in telephone networks ("The Shape of Phones" 2001)? What does it mean that, for consumer electronics firms, "building products that rely so much on technology from Microsoft and Intel runs counter to their culture" other than that few consumer electronics firms have been successful in the market for PCs based on Intel microprocessors and Microsoft software ("Gadget Wars" 2001)?

Two more examples will give a sense of the range of this sort of reference. Why would it be a change to its "armored-warrior culture" for the U.S. Army to adopt longer-range and unmanned weaponry as the central part of its arsenal instead of it being just a change to its arsenal, strategy, and tactics ("The Shape of the Battle" 2000)? And why will it take a "cultural revolution" for Oxford to make a success of its business school instead of just taking investment and time ("Dons and Dollars" 1996)?

Wittgenstein (1958, par. 614) famously asks: "What is left over if I subtract the fact that my arm goes up from the fact that I raise my arm?" The answer is his intention to raise his arm. Wittgenstein argues that this is fuzzy and vague and that philosophy would be better off to banish the idea. In the case of culture, the question that we must answer is of a different kind. For example: What is left over if we subtract the fact that the safety of Ontario Hydro's operations is rated "minimally acceptable" from the actions of the people in the company and the state of its equipment? The answer, apparently, is the organization's "safety culture." Culture is an extra factor offered in the explanation of Ontario Hydro's operational safety, just as intention is an extra factor offered in the explanation of Wittgenstein raising his arm.

Culture is no less fuzzy or vague than *intention,* and, in philosophical terms, Wittgenstein may be right that we would be better off banishing it from discussion. But, in ordinary language use, *intention* is important for assigning the causality of individual behavior and, therefore, predicting future behavior. That is how *culture* is being used here too: to assign causality to organizational behavior and to predict future organizational outcomes. In other words, it is being used to signal whether organizational outcomes were due to fortune or forces outside the organization's control or whether they were due to the organization itself and are, therefore, more likely to be sustainable. Describing an organization as "lack[ing] a strong safety culture" signals a belief that, if it has not had an accident yet, it is only because it has been lucky so far. Describing an organization as having a service culture indicates that any bad customer service that one might find is an exception and is likely to remain so in the future.

Similarly, we might say that describing the telephone industry as having a "switching" culture signals the belief that the failure of companies in that industry to adopt nonswitched technologies (such as "voice over Internet protocol") is not due to their not knowing about the new technologies, or to their not having gotten around to considering them, or to their having objectively assessed them and found them to be inferior to switching. It is due, instead, to something about organizations in this industry—their culture—that leads them to have a biased view about nonswitched technologies and causes them to believe that they are not viable. In this case, the bias is described as one of assumption and habit of thought and also of values: "Years of experience had taught the telephone engineers ('Bellheads,' to the trade) that only by switching whole lines to individual callers could they guarantee the quality of service deemed necessary" ("The Shape of Phones" 2001). The *value* is that only a very high level of service is acceptable. The *assumption* is that only by switching whole lines can this service be guaranteed. Together, these shut out other ways of thinking; they delegitimate alternatives. And, in so doing, they create inertia.

To say that changing a practice or a strategy will require the organization to change its culture, then, is to imply that the organization has a deeper commitment than usual to this practice or strategy. The army's adopting longer-range and unmanned weaponry as the central part of its arsenal is said to require a culture change because certain values of that organization, as represented by the high prestige given to "tankers," for example, and its assumptions about the need for "putting your young men in the mud" ("The Shape of the Battle" 2000) in order to defend or protect a land, commit it to the status quo. The reaction to the change is not rational, assumptions are not questioned, and values are not prioritized.

Likewise, to say that a culture change will be necessary for an organization to accommodate some new element (e.g., a strategy or a practice) is to imply that the new element conflicts with certain of the organization's existing commitments. The *Economist* argues (and, in a letter to the editor [*Economist*, 17 August 1996], two Oxford management professors write to disagree) that the introduction of a business school at Oxford conflicts with the values of the university—business studies is said to be held in low esteem there—and that the assumption that all faculty should be paid equally according to a rigid scheme will prevent the university from being able to lure high-profile faculty ("Dons and Dollars" 1996). In other words, commitment to the current salary scheme (or to the importance of tanks) may trump commitment to making a success of the business school (or to winning wars with minimal casualties).

We commonly discuss organizations in anthropomorphic terms, and it is common for the business press to describe management as the brains of the organization and labor as its brawn. When discussed abstractly, *culture* is sometimes analogized as the *personality* or the *identity* of the organization (e.g., "To Avoid a Job Failure" 1998). When we look at how it is used concretely, however, we see that *culture* plays more the role of the organization's *will*.

MANAGING CULTURE

That it does so inevitably raises the question: Do organizations have free will? Can the culture be managed? The business press betrays a strong bias toward a "great man" (or, occasionally, "great woman") theory of history when it comes to organizations and especially when it comes to organizational culture. Purposeful changes to organizational culture, or the lack thereof, are routinely attributed to the company's CEO or a small group of leaders under him or her. Therefore, the answer given in the business press is that, yes, culture can be managed. However, managing culture is considered exceedingly difficult, and, since there are no agreed-on guidelines for how it can be done and, where it has been done, very little clarity about how it has been done, those CEOs who are considered successful at it are described in heroic terms.

Noting that the importance of leadership in managing culture is well understood in large, established organizations, the *Economist* writes:

> However, it is also possible for leaders to define cultures in much younger organizations. It is noticeable that many of today's business heroes such as Richard Branson of Virgin and Anita Roddick of the Body Shop, are particularly talented at generating enthusiasm—and even passion—among their staff. . . .
>
> If your boss has a harried and hunted look as he travels the world pressing flesh and puffing egos, it may be because he is trying to do an impossible job. ("The Changing Nature" 1995)

CEOs who would manage the cultures of their organizations are said to face difficulties wherever they turn: "There is an increasing realization that corporate cultures are easy to destroy but difficult to create" ("Dusting the Opposition" 1995). That is, taking a "bad" culture and making it "good" (or making a good one better) is something that "takes years," even for heroes ("Lawyers Go Global" 2000). Meanwhile, good organizational cultures can go bad almost overnight, either because of the unintended consequences of managerial action or because of changes to the environment that make a once-successful culture suddenly inappropriate. Reporting about Yahoo!'s plunging stock price and bleak prospects, for example, the *Wall Street Journal* approvingly quotes an analyst who says: "Their culture helped them build a superb site and a really edgy brand, but it also held them back from making forward-looking business decisions. The culture that served them so incredibly well until the middle of last year is now letting them down." A once "cohesive" culture is now described as "insular" ("Insular Culture" 2001).

Like a battle going on in the mind of a dieter between the rational decision to lose weight and an uncooperative will when confronted with hunger or temptation, a battle between CEO and culture for supremacy in the organization is described. Writing about the appointment of Marjorie Scardino to head Pearson (which owns the *Economist*), the *Wall Street Journal* writes: "Famous among *Economist* staffers for her raw language and blunt approach, she says it's too early to say whether the Pearson culture is going to be hard to crack. 'To be honest, I don't yet know,' she says. 'I'm betting it's a culture I can deal with or change.' But the stock market is betting otherwise" ("Pearson Pins Hopes" 1996). Sometimes the battle is over quickly, like with C. T. Jenkins, who was fired after only three days because, as her termination report indicated, she was "too somber on the job" and decisions such as that to have lunch alone created "doubt that she would fit into the corporate culture" ("Many New Executives" 1994).

More often, however, the battle is protracted and its outcome uncertain until the very end. CEOs appointed from outside the company are scrutinized to see whether they understand enough of the culture that they are joining to be effective, and companies take great pains to reassure analysts that this is the case ("CEO to Go" 2000). "This guy understands our culture cold," the *Wall Street Journal* quotes the current Saatchi and Saatchi chairman and CEO as saying of his replacement, who had never even worked in the advertising industry ("Cordiant Picks Agency Novice" 1997).

On the other hand, CEOs appointed from within the company are scrutinized to see whether they have enough independence of thought to make a difference. The *Economist* wondered about Peter Salsbury, newly appointed chief executive of Marks and Spencer: "A bigger question is whether a man who has been steeped in the M&S culture for 28 years— his entire career—can distance himself sufficiently to take the difficult decisions that the group needs" ("Food for Thought" 1999). That question was resolved just over a year later when Mr. Salsbury resigned and was replaced by Luk Vandevelde, whom the *Economist* describes as "a well-known (if not famous) Belgian, fluent in five languages, [who] brings a foreign perspective and an outsider's insight that has been lacking at this very British company" ("Try, Try Again" 2000). Might Vandevelde be too much of an outsider, however? *The Times* puts the question most bluntly: "What does a Belgian know about a company as British as M&S?" "What, exactly, does a processed cheese magnate know about selling clothes?" ("The Big Cheese" 2000).

The question has yet to be decisively answered and likely will not be until either Marks and Spencer has a remarkable turnaround in financial performance or Vandevelde is forced to follow Salsbury and resign. The fog of war is dense during the battles between CEO and culture. Nothing can be said until the outcome is clear and history can be reconstructed for case studies and articles for the *Harvard Business Review*.

KNOWING CULTURE

Predictions of whether new CEOs will clash with the existing organizational culture raise the issue of how is it thought that we can characterize a culture: How do we come to know that it is bureaucratic, or innovative, or oddball? A similar question arises with the by-now de rigueur diagnoses of the potential for organizational culture clash in mooted mergers, acquisitions, and alliances.

Indeed, the two questions are often intertwined. I referred earlier to the case of *Paramount Communications, Inc. v. Time, Inc.* (1989), which has enshrined organizational culture in U.S. law. Delaware chancellor William T. Allen ruled that Time was within its rights when it sought to preserve its corporate culture by spurning a merger with Paramount in favor of one with Warner Communications. Time's culture was described by its management and board as being "in part pride in the history of the firm—notably Time Magazine and its role in American life—and in part a managerial philosophy and distinctive structure that is intended to protect journalistic integrity from pressures from the business side of the enterprise" (*13). Concretely, however, what was meant by maintaining a distinctive Time corporate culture was ensuring that Time's president, N. J. Nicholas, got the top job in the new firm—as Warner had agreed and Paramount would not. Chancellor Allen was not unaware of the possibility of cynicism in the case but, ultimately, sided with the argument of CEO as culture bearer. He wrote in his opinion:

> I note parenthetically that plaintiffs in this suit dismiss this claim of "culture" as being nothing more than a desire to perpetuate or entrench existing management disguised in a pompous highfalutin' claim. I understand the argument and recognize the risk of cheap deception that would be entailed in a broad and indiscriminate recognition of "corporate culture" as a valid interest that would justify a board in taking steps to defeat a non-coercive tender offer. Every reconfiguration of assets, every fundamental threat to the status quo, represents a threat to an existing corporate culture. But I am not persuaded that there may not be instances in which the law might recognize as valid a perceived threat to a "corporate culture" that is shown to be palpable (for lack of a better word), distinctive, and advantageous. (*13–*14)

The business press often takes the next step, moving from characterizing the CEO as managing and protecting the culture to characterizing the CEO as *standing for* the culture. In considering the cultural ramifications of the merger between Lockheed and Martin Marietta, the *Economist* wrote: "Yet some still wondered whether the two firms' cultures would gel, especially at the top. Mr. Tellep is the epitome of the southern Californian defense establishment: grey-suited, soft-spoken and with a penchant for politely avoiding the press (hardly surprising, perhaps, given the stories of bribes and cost overruns that had so often circled around Lockheed). In contrast, Mr. Augustine, a former Pentagon official, looks like a gruffer version of Sergeant Bilko—and is about as easy to keep silent" ("Engineering Dominance" 1995). Nothing more is said about the culture, the styles of the CEOs metonymically saying it all about the cultures.

What is more, it is not just the CEO who stands in for the culture as a whole. Sometimes it is the products of the organization, as in the case of the legal publishers Wasserstein acquiring National Law Publishing: "The purchase unites two very different cultures in legal publishing. The National Law Journal reports on legal issues with a broader scope touching on politics and business and is known as less sensationalistic than Wasserstein Perella's American Lawyer, which was founded by Steven Brill" ("Wasserstein Unit" 1997). Sometimes it is the incentive scheme of key employees—salary versus commission, for example ("Real-Estate Merger Wave" 1997). And sometimes it is the stereotyped aspirations and decisionmaking styles of those employees: "Business culture matters too. Investment bankers want to make lots of money and clear off; commercial bankers prefer a steadier career path. Commercial banks have slower, stodgier decision-making; investment bankers shoot from the hip. When commercial banks move into investment banking, the two cultures inevitably clash" ("Commercial Propositions" 1998).

Sometimes the customers that the organization serves stand in for the culture. Discussing Britain's newly merged financial regulator, the New Regulatory Organisation—or NewRO—which inherited the supervision of banking (from the Bank of England), insurance (from the Civil Service), and fund managers (from various self-regulatory organizations), the *Economist* reports: "The cultures of NewRO's constituent parts are as different as the industries they police: regulators of one-man financial-advisory outfits will sit side by side with supervisors of some of the biggest financial conglomerates in the world" ("Mr. Davies's NewROses" 1997). And sometimes it is even the company's logo, as with PanAmSat, the satellite company that proposed to merge with the Galaxy satellite business of Hughes Electronics: "The new merger may be a monumental culture clash: Hughes is a sober-suited business, while PanAmSat still plasters its launch vehicles with its founder's logo of a dog with its leg cocked" ("Activate the Money Star" 1997).

What all these examples point to is a sense that culture is cloudy and complicated but can be clarified and simplified by picking out a single artifact to stand for the whole. It is a rhetorical strategy, but it is also an epistemological one. The culture cannot be found except in the manifest artifacts that we can observe, and this strategy suggests that we search for the artifact that can serve as the master key, the metonymic element.

A more severe, but equally common, simplifying strategy is to identify a single adjective that can sum up the culture. We saw repeated examples of this earlier when examining assumptions about what makes for good and bad culture. In the cases of diagnoses of culture that are meant to determine the likelihood of postmerger indigestion, this reductionism is taken to extremes. Not only are cultures represented by single adjectives, but the selection of those adjectives is highly patterned. The *Wall Street Journal* sums up the potential culture clashes between BT and MCI as "Staid Brits Join Scrappy Yanks" ("BT Vaults into Ranks" 1996). Five months later, we learn that "Scrappy AOL, which has long focused on the consumer market, could clash with CompuServe's staid culture and its business-user base" ("AOL, CompuServe Shares" 1997). Apparently, these things come around every five months; next, it was the turn of Price Waterhouse and Coopers: "Besides differences over some financial issues, both have somewhat different cultures and personalities. Price Waterhouse, currently the sixth biggest accounting firm, is considered the old-line, white-shoe firm with the prestigious name, while No. 4 Coopers is viewed as the scrappier, more street-smart partnership" ("Coopers, Price Waterhouse" 1997).

Disappointed that we have only half the scrappy-staid formula? Fear not; the *Economist* comes to the rescue: "Another problem may be culture. E&Y and KPMG seem to be a more compatible couple than the free-wheeling Coopers and the slightly more staid Price Waterhouse" ("Bean-Counters Unite" 1997). Proving how hard it is to capture culture in a single word, this analysis proved to be wrong, as Price Waterhouse and Coopers merged while Ernst and Young and KPMG called off their merger because of culture issues. It turned out that it was "well known that Ernst partners are generally more entrepreneurial than the more buttoned-down KPMG partners, who tend to work with relatively risk-averse clients like the U.S. government" ("Ernst Blamed" 1998). It sounds as if Ernst and Young played Scrappy to KPMG's Staid.

Scrappy and Staid actually go by a number of names, but they are characters in a play reminiscent of Neil Simon's *The Odd Couple*, one that seems to structure thinking about cultures in merged organizations. It is the story of the conflicts that occur when an aggressive, street-smart, entrepreneurial, innovative, freewheeling, individualistic organization moves in with a conservative, buttoned-down, risk-averse, less dazzling, bureaucratic one.[5] As Simon might have asked, "Can two cultures share an organization without driving each other crazy?" From the point of view of BritArm, what is interesting is how often banks are cast in the role of the conservative, bureaucratic partner. Indeed, the *Wall Street Journal* quotes with approval an analyst who implies that banks epitomize the role: "It's always difficult to merge two separate cultures, particularly a bank and a highly entrepreneurial securities firm like Montgomery" ("Weisel's Quitting NationsBank" 1998).

Overall, this formulaic style of description gives the sense that organizational culture is straightforward and obvious to describe, that knowing a culture requires, not subtle empirical investigation, but, rather, just a quick

---

5. Examples of this story line include EDS and A. T. Kearney ("EDS Unit's Bid" 1995), Deutsche Bank and Morgan Grenfell ("Deutsche's Wayward Wunderkind" 1996), and Travelers Group and Salomon Inc. ("Salomon Succumbs" 1997).

look and a pick from the multiple choice of culture types. There is consensus that actually integrating the cultures of merged firms is very difficult and probably the most common cause of failed merger, but coming to know the culture is simple. More complex, nuanced newspaper accounts of organizational culture do exist, but they are rare, reserved mainly for postmortems of high-profile cases such as AT&T and NCR or Daimler-Chrysler where cultural integration is seen to have been a failure.[6]

Finally, there are articles that predict that a merger or an acquisition will create culture clash but that do not particularize the cultures in any way. "The two groups have totally different cultures," says the *Wall Street Journal* without elaboration about the French retailers Promodes and Casino ("Promodes Ups the Stakes" 1997). "Many analysts, though, speculate that the deal was condemned to fail by conflicting corporate cultures," says the *Economist* of Monsanto and AHP with equal brevity ("It Ain't Necessarily So" 1998). We might infer from examples such as these that culture is so complex that it cannot be accurately ascertained quickly—even by so observant an outsider as a journalist—or at least that it cannot be conveniently simplified in a short newspaper account. Many of these empty descriptions of culture, however, have the flavor exemplified by this report about Vodafone-Mannesmann: "Everybody expects Vodafone to have huge problems integrating its networks and culture with those of Mannesmann" ("What Next?" 2000). Culture, now as real a part of the organization as its technology, is described in the same terms: something trivial to see, although very tricky to manage.

ORGANIZATIONS AND NATIONAL CULTURE

The final theme of organizational culture pertains to national or regional organizational cultures. Although the same instrumental approach to culture applies, references to the corporate or business culture of an entire nation or continent tend to be somewhat more cautious than are those to a mere organization. The *Economist* never qualifies its summary judgments about individual organizational cultures, but, in its survey of American business, it writes: "Talk about America's 'business culture' sounds pretentious. A lot of things ascribed to culture boil down to particular legal and financial arrangements. But there is something more to it. American businessmen seem to attach special value to novelty and individualism" ("Back on Top?" 1995). It is somewhat less apologetic about

---

6. For an example of the broad claim that it is poor cultural integration that leads most mergers to fail, see "Why Too Many Mergers" (1997). On AT&T and NCR, see "Why AT&T Takeover" (1995) and "Fatal Attraction" (1996). On Daimler and Chrysler, see "Chrysler-Daimler" (1998) and "The DaimlerChrysler Emulsion" (2000).

referring to Japan's "dozy corporate culture" ("Ever So Polite" 2001) and its "rigid corporate culture" ("Doing It Differently" 1997). Likewise, it does not hide its impatience with Germany's "corporate culture that favors consensus and the interests of 'stakeholders' over those of shareholders" ("Mobile Warfare" 1999), with the "flaws in Italy's corporate culture" (namely, cronyism and lack of transparency) ("Flattering to Deceive" 2001), or with the fact that "British business culture [is] more fearful of failure" than is the American ("Ripe for Picking" 1999). The *Wall Street Journal* weighs in with an op-ed piece discussing the reasons that privatization has not made Russian firms more competitive: "Part of the problem is well-known and can be summed up as a Soviet-style management culture that is biased against innovation, risk-taking and investment" ("Ridding Russia" 1996).

These country corporate cultures are not defended or explained in detail: they are assumed to be well-known to readers and to express the consensus view. Individual organizations are then assessed in terms of how close they are to or how far they are from the overall business culture of their home country. The *Economist* writes: "In many cases, a company's culture is bound up with its home country" ("Europe's Businesses" 1997). So, for example, "although both operate worldwide, the culture of General Motors is distinctively American, that of Volkswagen identifiably German" ("Worldbeater, Inc." 1997). The fact that the "cockpit culture" of Korean Air was too Korean—that is, so authoritarian that the copilot did not question the captain even though there was confusion in the cockpit—was blamed for the crash of Flight 801 in 1997 ("Korean Air Tries" 1999). This is in contrast to the situation at Hoechst, which has "de-Germanified" itself so much that "about the only thing German about Hoechst AG these days is its name." Its chairman boasts that it is now "a nonnational company" ("How a Chemicals Giant" 1997).

Teles, on the other hand, also German by birth, is said to be not so much nonnational as admirably American in its culture, especially in its "conception of hard work" ("German Lessons" 1997). And Nokia is described as having struck a good balance. It is "the very antithesis of the ugly multinational . . . : Finland's egalitarian corporate culture is just the sort of thing that management gurus are prescribing for companies everywhere. But the company also does everything it can to encourage a resolutely global mindset" ("To the Finland Base Station" 1999).

Here, we find the general normative message of the American and British business press about national organizational culture: avoid being too close to the stereotype of your national corporate culture. Whether you are British, French, German, Russian, or Japanese, probably the less you are like your national corporate culture, the better. If American (or Finnish), then you come from a national corporate culture close to the ideal. Just don't overdo it. Although European and Asian companies are praised for being more American, when American companies are referred to as *American*, it is generally because they are being stereotypically American in their ignorance or insensitivity to other cultures—as in the case of Disney in France ("The Kingdom" 1996) or Nike in Brazil and Britain ("As In-Your-Face Ads Backfire" 1997). The message presupposes, then, that lay ethnography at the organizational level should take into account lay ethnography of the home country in a judgmental way and lay ethnography of other countries in a nonjudgmental way: keep only what is good of your home country's corporate culture; understand other national cultures well enough to fit in and do business there.

SUMMARY

So what can we say in summary about the idea of culture that day to day, or week to week, the business press reinforces? First, there is a clear theory in use about what sort of cultures are good or bad for organizations. This theory is grounded in a contingency model, but assumptions about homogeneity make it a contingency theory with very little contingency. Bureaucratic culture epitomizes the negative ideal of organizational culture; its opposite—the entrepreneurial, innovative, risk-accepting, cohesive organizational culture—is the positive. The link between culture and performance is, however, complex. If an organization's culture strays in too obvious a fashion from the presumed ideal, it will be described in negative terms even if the organization's performance is good. On the other hand, an organizational culture that seems close to the ideal will be redescribed in negative terms if the organization's performance is bad enough.

In general, culture is invoked analogously to the way in which intention or will is: to signal beliefs about whether observed behavior is best explained by endogenous or exogenous causes—that is, whether the organization itself or forces outside it (including luck or fortune) deserve the credit or the blame for outcomes—and to indicate predictions of future behavior. Managing culture is considered very difficult, a black art practiced by heroes, not a science or a technical skill that can be learned by just anyone. Accurately describing a culture is, however, straightforward once its master key has been found. The cultures of particular organizations will vary more or less from the generic corporate culture of their home countries. No matter where you are from, the secret—at least according to the British and American press—is to be American, but not too American.

Usage in BritArm

During my fieldwork in BritArm, I found that managers drew on the business press usage of *culture* believingly but selectively. In particular, the connotations of *culture* in the Bank had three typical characteristics. First, abstract discussions about the definition of *culture* were rare, and those that I did encounter may sometimes have been prompted by my presence. More often, *culture* was used as if its meaning were self-evident. The fuzzy, ambiguous, implicit definition that results causes little apparent confusion or misunderstanding.

Second, the culture of the Bank is always described in negative terms. Local "subcultures" are sometimes described positively—usually to contrast them with the mainstream—but I never heard anyone espouse the desirability of the organization's culture or discuss it in purely neutral terms. It is described as too bureaucratic, too rules driven, not customer focused enough, not entrepreneurial enough, too inflexible, too prone to navel gazing, too centralized. In other words, it is the very epitome of the negatively ideal organizational culture. It is also described as fitting two cultural stereotypes almost perfectly: that of being a bank and that of being British. There is pride taken in its being British and self-importance drawn from its being a bank. But it is considered too British and too bank-like for its own good. These truths are, generally, considered to be self-evident.

Third, culture is assumed to be difficult to change. Indeed, inertia serves as culture's defining characteristic. Thus, undesirable habits or attitudes or preferences can be labeled part of the culture as shorthand to indicate their being resistant to change, and one of the most straightforward uses of the idea of culture is to explain (account for or diagnose) an unfortunate lack of change. As I describe in the next chapter, whether the explanation is couched as an account or as a diagnosis depends on the speaker's opinion of the practical possibility of changing the culture at all given the context. There is great cynicism about the degree to which the executives of the Bank have the heroic qualities necessary to lead a change of culture within it.

Although the lay ethnography in BritArm certainly reflects the messages about organizational culture conveyed by the business press, it would be wrong to say that it is determined by them. The meanings of popular culture messages—even when they concern the idea of culture itself—are always negotiated. These messages are one more part of the situation that confronts members of a culture or subculture and that they will come to make sense of using the cultural meanings that they have to hand. Obscure when discussed abstractly like this, the process will become clear in the next two chapters as I examine concretely how the people in BritArm makes sense of their culture while it makes sense of them and how they use it to achieve their ends while also being used.

Usage in This Book

In defining my own idea of culture, the idea that informs this book and that has shaped the questions asked and the answers given, I take my cue from two ethnographers: John Van Maanen and Pierre Bourdieu. Both argue, in different ways, against abstract definitions of *culture* and for contextualized ones even though (or, more accurately, because) this will lead to a proliferation of idiosyncratic conceptions of culture, one per study. They argue, in other words, that the same lack of necessary consensus that makes *culture* so useful in ordinary language also makes it useful in academic writing, although for very different reasons. Van Maanen puts it this way: "The ends of fieldwork involve the catchall idea of culture; a concept as stimulating, productive, yet fuzzy to fieldworkers and their readers as the notion of life is for biologists and their readers" (Van Maanen 1988, 3). In other words, concrete descriptions of particular cultures are best served by vague definitions of culture in general. Ethnography is, after all, an inductive endeavor. Keeping culture imprecise in the abstract encourages each ethnographer to arrive inductively at a conception of culture appropriate for the context studied—or, indeed, to avoid defining *culture* altogether and using more limited and specific terms instead. Many anthropologists seem to share this sentiment: ethnographies regularly lack abstract definitions of *culture*, and, even in Clifford and Marcus's celebrated collection of essays *Writing Culture* (1986), there is not a single definition of the term.

Bourdieu (in Bourdieu and Wacquant 1992, 22) agrees that avoiding precise definitions should be an explicit sociological strategy. He claims that culture—or *habitus*, to use his term—is "in cahoots with the fuzzy and the vague" and that to define it precisely is of no more use for theory than it is for description. Those of us who struggle at times to make sense of Bourdieu's prose in English translation may sometimes cynically feel that he is making a virtue of necessity, but he argues as follows: "The peculiar difficulty of sociology, then, is to produce a precise science of an imprecise, fuzzy, wooly reality. For this it is better that its concepts be polymorphic, supple, and adaptable, rather than defined, calibrated, and used rigidly" (23). Eschewing the "ostentatious rigor" that he finds all too common in anthropology and sociology, he says later: "Ideally, one would like to be able completely to avoid talking about concepts for their own sake and so running the risk of being both schematic and formal. Like all dispositional concepts, the concept of the habitus, which is predisposed by its range of historical uses to designate a system of acquired, permanent, generative dispositions, is justified above all by the false problems and false solutions that it eliminates, the questions it enables one to formulate better or to resolve, and the specifically scientific difficulties to which it gives rise" (290). In other words, the quality of a definition ought to be determined by its practical usefulness in ethnography (Van Maanen) and theory (Bourdieu), not by its clarity, precision, or elegance. And, above all, the appropriate place for that discussion is in the midst of that ethnography or theory, with a clear conception being its end, not its precursor.

For the purposes of this study, we may say abstractly that culture is the patterned expression—in words and behaviors and artifacts—of the social distribution of modes of thought—assumptions, values, interpretive schemas, know-how, and so on—of a group of people. This formulation is borrowed from Hannerz (1992, 7), and it reflects two important assumptions about culture that underlie the analysis in the following chapters.

The first of these assumptions is that cultures in organizations are not monolithic: they are imperfectly shared. Even the most gray-flannel-suited organization man (or whoever may stand in as today's equivalent to Wilson's [1955] and Whyte's [1956] classic characterizations) is an individual. New members arrive at an organization with a cultural identity (or more than one) already mostly formed. As they are socialized into the organization, they learn more and more of the new culture, but, likely, they never learn it all, and seldom do they accept everything that they have learned. Thus, culture is socially distributed across the organization—and typically unevenly so—and this distribution can be expected to change over time.

The second assumption is that culture is a social phenomenon that exists only insofar as it is continually produced and reproduced by individuals in the group. Culture is not "out there" except insofar as it is also "in here." Culture may be embedded in objects or symbols, but it requires an interpreting mind to have meaning and to be enacted. It is the jointly produced public expression of assumptions, interpretations, skills, and other modes of thought held privately by individuals. Thus, culture has both macro- and micro-level loci.

This is a generic definition, and it may raise as many questions about culture as it answers. The point of Van Maanen's and Bourdieu's argument is that such answers come less persuasively from abstract theorizing than from concrete analysis of particular cases. To understand what this definition of *culture* means and why its entailing assumptions are warranted and significant—to understand what *culture* means and how culture works—we need to get off the slippery ice of abstraction and back to what Geertz (2000, xii), neatly quoting Wittgenstein, calls *the rough ground*. It is time to use the friction of ethnography to give us some traction. In the next chapter, I examine concretely the derogations, deprecations, accounts, and diagnoses that make up the negative lay ethnography in BritArm and look at the different uses to which each is put as people try to make sense of, and get ahead in, the Bank.

Modes and forms

When two Englishmen meet, their first talk is of the weather.
—Samuel Johnson

Everyone talks about the weather, but
nobody does anything about it.
—Mark Twain

Retail banks are not much loved. They offer one set of services—the taking of deposits and the handling of payments—that people are disinclined to pay for and another—lending at rates of interest to individuals and small businesses—that carries ancient connotations of immorality and exploitation. Judaism, Christianity, and Islam have all at one time had strictures against charging interest, or *usury*, as the practice is known pejoratively, among coreligionists. Islam maintains them to this day. The taking of interest was illegal in Great Britain until 1545, and the courts there can still hold a given rate to be injurious, a power that they do not wield over most prices. Marxist economic theory views interest as money for nothing, the exploitation of the poor by the rich, and echoes of this argument can be heard in the current-day popular protests against the World Bank and in favor of debt relief for Third World nations.

Medieval banking in Europe—essentially moneylending—was dominated by Jews, who were not subject to Christian laws against usury and who were, moreover, prohibited from practicing most other occupations. It is unclear whether this connection between Jews and moneylending, famously realized in Shakespeare's Shylock in *The Merchant of Venice*, did more to increase the prejudice against Jews or the resentment against usurers, but a distrust of banks that has its origins in anti-Semitism persisted into the twentieth century and is not entirely absent today. More widely resonant than the portrayal of Shylock in modern America and Britain, however, may be the words of Polonius in act 1, scene 3, of *Hamlet:*

Neither a borrower, nor a lender be;
For loan oft loses both itself and friend,
And borrowing dulls the edge of husbandry.

Nevertheless, even if banking is no longer stigmatized and is by now squarely part of the establishment in capitalist societies, it is still seen as lacking a certain virtue. Further, it is demeaning to have to ask for a loan and then be forced to provide the intimate details of one's financial situation and to have one's ability to repay questioned. It is deeply embarrassing to ask and then be turned down. Banks are like universities in this one important respect: they not only serve their customers; they judge them.

If banks are resented when they make large profits, they suffer an even worse image problem when they lose money. When loans cannot be repaid and must be foreclosed, it is typically the banks that are seen as the guilty party as they repossess property taken as security, that is, take their pound of flesh. Because they lend at long terms of repayment but promise to repay deposits on demand, their viability depends on trust. Banks are ruined when depositors decide en masse to withdraw their funds. Thus, they have long jealously guarded their reputations for reliability and conservatism. Despite federal deposit insurance in the United States and the fact that runs on banks are no longer a part of living memory for most Americans or Britons, few people want to deposit their money in an exciting or idiosyncratic bank—even, or perhaps especially, in this Internet Age. Nor do they want to deposit their money in a bank that looks poor enough that it may go out of business any day. Banks and bankers should be boring. That is the way we prefer them. And banks should be rich (even if most of their employees are not well paid). That is why we can trust them with our money. But it is also why we hate them for charging us, why public resentment is so high when banks impose charges for using a competitor's ATM or for services performed in a branch.

Bankers are, thus, seen as both less than virtuous and less than interesting. Being perceived as a bit bad yet basically boring is unusual. Most occupations considered to include an element of vice also hold a degree of public fascination. Not retail banking. Soldiers and spies, cops and lawyers, politicians and prostitutes, even investment bankers, all are regular fare in novels, movies, and television. Retail bank managers barely feature as extras. It is inconceivable, for example, to imagine a banker feeling the need to come forward to say that, really, the job isn't as glamorous as Hollywood makes it out to be, as police officers and former intelligence officers periodically do. With the possible exception only of accountancy and actuarial science, there is no occupation portrayed in duller terms than branch banking.

I must confess that, when starting this study, I shared this perception of banks being dull places. In fact, I felt studying one to be something of a source of status deprivation among other ethnographers. Sociologists are denied the exoticism taken for granted by anthropologists. Still, we can study deviants and drug users, doctors and drunk drivers; we can observe tearooms and insane asylums. And almost anything seemed more exciting to me than observing behavior in a bank. Within organizational ethnography, I found myself jealous of those who studied the police and prisoners of war, factory floors and nuclear power plants, the making of high-tech computers and high-tech trains. Even studying funeral directors and bill collectors seemed fascinating for the chance to be around dead bodies and deadbeats.[7] But a bank?

Yet I decided to study BritArm. As an American who had lived in England for three years, who is married to a British woman, who was struck by the fascinating play of difference and similarity between the cultures of the United States and the United Kingdom, but who had never actually worked in Britain, I wanted to study a British company. As I described in chapter 2, through the auspices of MIT, where I was a doctoral student, BritArm offered me access as a researcher in return for my promise to "hold a mirror up" to the company at the end of my study, to help it see its culture through the eyes of an outsider who did not share its basic assumptions and who might, therefore, reveal what had always been taken for granted.

The people I met from the Bank seemed to me to be exceedingly nice and thoughtful, and the nicer they were to me, the more accessible they made themselves to my observations, and the more I involved me as a member of their community, the more I felt terrible about having worried that they would be boring. The truth is, of course, that, just as police work is sometimes as exciting as imagined but usually less so, so is banking sometimes as dull as imagined but usually (somewhat) less so. But the guilt that I felt did not stem from having been wrong. Before I met her, my wife had been a management trainee at Lloyds Bank, so I was prepared for the idea that some of the jobs in the Bank would be stereotypically dull but many would not, that some of the people in the Bank would be stereotypically

7. On deviants and drug users, see Becker (1997). On doctors, see Bosk (1992). On drunk drivers, see Gusfield (1981). On tearooms, see Humphreys (1970). On insane asylums, see Goffman (1961a). On the police, see Van Maanen (1975). On prisoners of war, see Schein (1961). On factories, see Burawoy (1979). On nuclear power plants, see Perrow (1984). On computer engineers, see Perlow (1997). On the making of high-tech trains, see Latour (1996). On funeral directors, see Barley (1983). And, finally, on bill collectors, see Sutton (1991). This list is not definitive in any way, except as a sample of those researchers of whom I was jealous while I was in the field and whose work I admire.

gray but many would not. Rather, my self-criticism stemmed from realizing that no group of people was more aware of how boring they and their jobs were thought to be than the people who worked for BritArm. In such a circumstance, to join the chorus of outside voices reminding them how boring is banking was not just offensive; it was, well, boring.

I began to see in myself a set of assumptions about good occupations and bad occupations to observe, good organizations and bad organizations to study. I began to question why it seemed so natural to disclaim the boring, the staid, the risk averse, the traditional, in organizations. Now, I am not suggesting that we need to adopt a new politically correct term to replace *boring*—the *differently interesting to be around*, or something similar— but let me try an analogy to other forms of prejudice. It is one thing to feel guilty because you assign someone to a category only to learn later that he does not fit it. It is another to feel guilty at your relief that he does not fit it. It is the difference between feeling guilty that you thought your daughter's boyfriend was a British banker when he is not and feeling guilty that it bothered you so much that he might have been. The first is an error of categorization; the second is a prejudice. I regretted my prejudice, and I began to realize the frame trap (Goffman 1974, 480) facing those who work for organizations widely considered to be boring: if they disagree and say that they don't think that the work there is boring, their disagreement is taken as evidence, not about the organization, but about *them*. They must be boring to find that kind of thing interesting.

When I first arrived in London to begin my fieldwork, I had a long conversation with an immigration official at Passport Control at Heathrow Airport. Because I was staying for a year, I could not enter the country on a tourist visa and had to demonstrate that I was there on legitimate business, that I had sufficient funding for the year and so was not going to seek work, and so on. My wife being British, I could have applied for a work permit, but doing so was not necessary and would have required additional paperwork. I had all my documents in order, including my letter of introduction from a BritArm executive, but the immigration official was dubious. "BritArse?[8] What are you studying them for?" she asked. I explained my project in vague terms as a study of the Bank's management practices. "Right. So you're interested in what *not* to do." I chuckled, but she wasn't smiling and hadn't stamped my passport yet, so I meekly agreed. "Well, you should have a word with them about my overdraft," she said as she finally did stamp my passport and waved me to go ahead. "Scandalous."

---

8. *BritArse* is a substitute for the actual (commonly heard in England) play on the Bank's real name repeated then by the agent.

I got a similar reaction from nearly every member of the British public to whom I described my research. Employees experience this too: so much so that female staff in London complained that they felt uncomfortable riding on the underground in their BritArm uniforms because they feared harassment. Not sexual harassment (the uniforms seemed designed not to encourage that at least) but "Oh, so you work for BritArm, do you?" harassment. The idea that the Bank might be full of hardworking, well-intentioned people doing a dirty job in ingenious ways that had been developed over the years and from which other organizations might learn a lot was dismissed out of hand by my British friends. Anyone who hadn't been living under a rock—or in the United States—would know how crazy *that* was, I was told. And don't feel sorry for them. Do you know how much money they made last year?

This is not unique to BritArm. "Most people dislike banks," writes the *Economist* of the British, "because of what they perceive to be arrogance, unfair charges, errors and poor service" ("Love Me" 2002). All the major "High Street banks" (as the large retail banks are known in Britain) have similar public images. I quickly learned that, if the banks made poor profits, it was a sign of how badly run they were and that, if they made high profits, it was a sign of how badly they exploited their customers.[9]

The fact was that I had not chosen to study BritArm because I thought that it represented some kind of best practice and that the audience that I hoped might be able to learn something from my description of the organization consisted, not of managers in other organizations, but, rather, of academics. Nevertheless, outside the organization I found myself feeling increasingly defensive and protective of BritArm as my time with the Bank went along, even as inside the organization I was getting more and more able to join in the jokes and complaints at the Bank's expense. The typical cure for going native is going home, at least for a while. I tried that more than once (my wife had stayed behind in Boston, so it was a cure for more than one ailment). This particular strain, however, was immune to that treatment. It was not that, living in the organization, I was becoming brainwashed by positive images of the Bank. Far from it. It was that, the more teasing and complaining about the Bank I was able to join in with

9. In this way, the banks are treated similarly to another great British institution, the British Broadcasting Corp. The BBC is seen as a national treasure in a way that the banks most certainly are not. The public reaction to the announcement of the BBC's ratings, however, is very reminiscent of the reaction to the announcement of bank profits. If the ratings are too low, the BBC is criticized for being increasingly irrelevant. If the ratings are too high, it is criticized for kowtowing to the masses. Or at least this is how things are seen by its director-general, Greg Dyke, who once commented: "This is an unusual job. It's not often that you get criticized for losing and you get criticized for winning" ("What Price Success" 2002). Perhaps it is less unusual than he suspects.

people inside the organization, the less teasing and complaining I wanted to hear from people outside it.

Perhaps ethnography is always participant-observation in the sense that what ethnographers learn from observing during their time in the field depends very much on what happens to them as individuals during that time. Doubtless, my own concerns that I was prejudiced in favor of some organizational cultures as interesting to study and others as not led me to wonder more generally about the existence of biases toward and against certain forms of organizational culture. Having to cope myself with public negativity toward BritArm when a small piece of my identity was tied up with the organization made me attentive to the ways in which full members of the organization—how much they identify with the Bank being itself an empirical question for me—coped with that issue. Inevitably, the issues that *I* faced are the ones that I noticed *them* most keenly having to face, and this ethnography—for better and worse—reflects that.

From observing the reactions within BritArm to the negative external commentary with which its employees are bombarded, I noticed that there are three patterns of response. First of all, there is no tolerance in the Bank for outside voices claiming that the banking business is inherently exploitative. There is tremendous frustration when people—especially journalists—do not seem to understand how important banking is to society; when they seem not to value services such as check writing and cashpoint machines (ATMs) and to take for granted that these should be offered for free; and when they do not understand the risks of the business, especially the risks of lending money (i.e., when loans are repaid, banks earn only interest, but, when loans go bad, they lose both interest and principal, one bad loan therefore wiping out the profits earned by many, many others). Second, there is much variation in how people in the Bank respond to particular complaints about the service that they provide to customers. This varies on a case-by-case basis and also by individual. Some people are more likely to take the Bank's side, others to sympathize with the customer. Third, there is almost uniform agreement with negative comments about the culture of the Bank, about how it is run, about its management style, about the fact that it is bureaucratic, staid, risk averse, and boring. That is not to say that people in BritArm appreciate hearing such comments from outsiders—far from it. But such comments are echoed in the jokes and complaints heard everywhere inside the Bank.

Let me give an example. Seven months into my fieldwork, I was in London interviewing various people in BritArm's Head Office. Arriving one day for an interview with an executive, I was met by a member of his

staff, Ben, a senior manager, who told me that there would be a delay before the interview got started but suggested that, in the meantime, if I
would follow him, he would take me to a conference room and maybe he
could start to answer some of my questions. As he led me into the stuffy
conference room, he walked over to open the window. It promptly fell
shut. He fiddled with the mechanism, but he could not get the window to
stay open. "BritArm technology," he said with a smile as he gave up and
sat down. "Now, let me tell you a little bit about myself."

By this time, I had been in the Bank long enough to know that Ben had
already told me a little bit about himself and also about how he viewed
me. Small jokes at the Bank's expense are common conversational icebreakers in BritArm. They draw people together with their allusion to
shared experience. They put people at ease with one another through the
comforting routine of their recital. BritArm employees complain about
the Bank in the same way that the British public complains about the
weather: incessantly and with good humor. And, as with gripes about the
weather, these little jibes about the Bank prompt quick agreement but do
not by themselves signal antagonism. Ben's quip about the Bank's technology was no more a call for something to be done or an expression of
deep frustration than his earlier greeting to me, "How do you do?" was a
request for a medical report or an expression of deep concern about my
health.

What had Ben told me with his derogatory remark? He told me of
affinity with the Bank, not alienation from it. He displayed an agility with
the Bank's culture, not a peevishness about its technology. And he told me
that I was not viewed as hostile, that I was seen as at least a partial insider.

This episode reveals both the depth and the shallowness of the culture
of complaint in BritArm. That culture runs deep enough to shape even
patterns of casual greeting in the Bank and to lead to a BritArm reading
of elements of British culture. Complaints, however, can be superficial
and sometimes do not correspond to feelings of deep discontent. Other
times they do, of course. What I want to do in this chapter is to distinguish
among several modes and forms of negative expression about the Bank
and examine the uses and effects of each as well as the cultural competence required to employ each effectively and the sanctions against their
misuse. The idea is to see how this patterned negativity serves to reinforce
the established order: the boring, bureaucratic culture that is so often
itself the target of the negativity. Although on one level the negativity
serves to amplify the external criticism of the Bank, on another level it is
a way of coping with that criticism without provoking change.

The typology that I propose to help make sense of the manifestations

CHAPTER FOUR / 64

of negative expression proceeds from two distinctions, distinctions that can be summarized as follows:

| | FORM OF EXPRESSION | |
MODE OF THOUGHT	Criticism	Explanation
Acquiescent	Derogation	Account
Antagonistic	Deprecation	Diagnosis

The first distinction is between expressions formed as *criticisms* and those couched as *explanations*. This is the difference between expressions considered to be subjective opinions and those considered to be objective descriptions, respectively. The question, Considered so by whom? is relevant since, as we shall see, there are interesting cases of disagreement on this point between speakers and various members of their audience. The second distinction is between modes of thought *antagonistic* toward some aspect of the current situation and those *acquiescent* to the status quo. When applied to an expression formed as a criticism, this distinction is the difference between a *deprecation*, "an earnest desire that something may be averted or removed," and a *derogation*, "a lowering of honor or esteem," respectively.[10] In other words, it is the difference between a call for redress and a put-down. When applied to an expression formed as an explanation, the distinction is the difference between a *diagnosis* of why the Bank is failing to meet its goals and an *account* of why things are the way they are, respectively. For example, it is the difference between an identification of why an area of the Bank is not reaching its potential and an account of why the potential of that area is not as great as one might think. An essential characteristic of these categories is that there is no unequivocal partition between them—these distinctions are in play in the Bank. They are conceptually distinct, but the ambiguity between them has important tactical consequences, which I will discuss.

Derogations

Ben's joke about BritArm technology was a derogation. This is because it was a criticism—it put the Bank down—but did not express a deprecation's "earnest desire" for change. Instead, it signaled a passive, resigned acceptance of the window's closing and the state of the Bank's technology as things that, for the time being, we were going to have to live with. It is in this sense that we can say that Ben was expressing acquiescence to

10. These definitions come from *The Oxford English Dictionary*.

the status quo. This is not to say that he did not possess a desire that the Bank's technology and window fittings improve; it is merely to say that he did not express that desire to me at that time. His remark was not a solicitation of redress but a way to make me laugh, to put me at ease, and to warm up our conversation.

This might sound obvious, and it would almost certainly be obvious to BritArm employees, for whom the use of derogatory remarks to produce these sorts of desirable social outcomes is well established. Such a practice is not universal, however, not even in banks. It is culturally specific. For example, in his ethnography of the Japanese retail bank Uedagin, Rohlen (1974, 50) describes how "love Uedagin" is considered the proper attitude toward the company and how employees are expected to dramatize that attitude through expressions of "pride, dedication, and enthusiastic participation." In such a context, derogation of the bank can be expected to lead to frowns, unease, and coolness—except when voiced among intimates. It is a form of expression that *presupposes* intimacy rather than strengthening it. This is a difference of organizational culture, but it reflects national cultural differences as well. The British are generally more comfortable than the Japanese are with self-mockery and rather less comfortable with displays of patriotism or enthusiastic participation. In their use of derogatory remarks about the Bank to break the conversational ice, employees of BritArm are enacting British culture, but in a particularly BritArm way.

LEARNING HOW TO DEROGATE

As one example of how derogation plays out in BritArm, consider the following from my time with Cutler and the others in the Securities Centre introduced in chapter 2. After I had been sitting alongside Cutler for two weeks learning the intricacies of his role as a doer 2 at the Securities Centre, he asked if I would like to be a "huge help" to him and his colleagues on Team 2. I was put on my guard by the sly grin on his face and the conspiratorial glances that he shared with those sitting nearby. But I was enthusiastic about the prospect of ingratiating myself to a useful informant and of shifting my fieldwork to *participant*-observation. I readily agreed.

The task that Cutler had in mind for me was the revaluation of a portfolio of shares lodged with the Bank by a customer to secure a line of credit. It was not urgent: the job had been left undone for over a month. But it was required by the Bank's internal auditors, and Cutler did not know when he would be able to find time to do it. The job was tedious. Cutler retrieved for me the customer's file, which contained hundreds of share certificates from over 120 different companies.

It is worth a brief digression to point out that, in the Securities Centres, documents are stored, not in file folders, but, rather, in A4-sized envelopes slit open across the top. These are called *pods,* and, on the way to retrieve the files on this day, I asked Cutler why. "I don't know," he told me. "Stupid, isn't it?" Derogations can be used, not just as icebreakers to get conversations started, but also as deflections to bring conversations—and inquiry—to an end.

Looking through the relevant file, figuring out what was what, was difficult because companies represented in the portfolio had merged, been acquired, gone bankrupt, or changed names over the years. It took me the rest of the day merely to produce a list of which current share prices I needed to obtain. Normally, when shares are taken by the Bank as security, they are held in a central department that takes care of revaluations. This customer was an exception for reasons no one at the Securities Centre knew.

I had to write the list out in longhand since the computers on our desks were not equipped for doing word-processing or spreadsheet work. Two of the eighty computers in the Centre did have Microsoft Word and Excel on them, but I was advised that it was best just to do the job by hand. This was frustrating since the customer's file contained a computer print-out of the previous valuation from two years ago. It would have saved time and effort had I been able to start with the original computer file and make additions and modifications to it. All I had, however, was the print-out, so I would have had to retype it all regardless.

Members of the team paid me a lot of attention while I worked away at the revaluation. Nick, the team leader, came by a number of times to see how I was getting on and to show his appreciation. After a couple of hours, Cutler apparently started to feel guilty about having given me so much to do. "You've gone awfully quiet over there," he said. Our desks were head to head in a line with other desks in the open-plan office. "You know, you don't have to do it," he added. "Just leave it, and I can finish it later." I assured him that I didn't mind. "But it's very boring. You must be bored out of your mind over there." Not wanting to complain, I said that I was all right with it, that it was good to have a little job to do. "Yeah, but it's pretty tedious, isn't it?" I demurred, but, after several people stopped by over the course of the afternoon to sympathize and tell me how boring the work that I was doing was, I confessed, yes, it was fairly tedious. "Oh, I know," I was told.

The floor under the desk I was sitting at had a slight tilt to it, not uncommon in old English buildings. It meant that my chair kept slowly sliding away from the desk and that I had to keep scooting myself in all the time. It was uncomfortable, and Cutler noticed me fiddling around with the chair adjustments to see whether I could stop from rolling back. "Uncomfortable, isn't it?" he said. I agreed, complaining that my back was starting to hurt from all this scooting and sliding. He and Joan, the doer 1 sitting next to him, laughed and said that they had each used to sit over on that side but had switched desks for precisely that reason. We complained convivially about the conditions under which we were forced to work, and I said that I didn't know how Tom—the man whose desk I was borrowing—put up with it. It transpired that Tom had previously been a coal miner, so this deprivation was likely pretty mild by his standards. Indeed, it was mild by most any standard and certainly by the historical standards of British clerical work. The occupational physician Charles Turner Thackrah, for example, observed of bank clerks in 1831 that they "suffered from the confined atmosphere [of the counting house], a fixed position and often from long days": "Their muscles are often distressed by the maintenance of one posture and they complain frequently of pains in the side of the chest. The digestive organs suffer most, a fact apparent even from the countenance and tongue. The circulation is imperfect; the head becomes affected and though urgent disease is not generally produced, yet a continuance of the employment in its fullest extent never fails to impair the constitution and render the individual sickly for life" (quoted in Anderson 1976, 17). And, to some extent, the fact that my discomfort was minor, but nevertheless real, was exactly the point.

Encouraged by this friendly banter, I went on to make derogatory remarks about how ridiculous it was to do this by hand, about the state of the brush in my bottle of correcting fluid, and about the customer who, I hypothesized aloud, didn't actually need the line of credit but just opened it so that we would be the custodian of his shares. Joan and Cutler seemed to find my exasperation hilarious, and Joan told me: "Now you know what it is like to be a BritArm securities clerk." This struck me. If she was right, then being a securities clerk at BritArm feels like basking in the warm glow of adversity with sympathizers all around. I felt more like a part of the team than I ever had before, and the event marked a turning point in my relationship with Team 2. Afterward, team members treated me with less suspicion and more like one of their own. To have suffered enough to be able to complain about the Bank was to be part of the group, and to have made these mild derogations was evidence of my bona fides, evidence that I was "all right."

As I was being socialized to understand, derogation is an important element of the culture at BritArm. The ritual of making derogatory remarks about some aspect of the Bank and receiving empathy in return, and perhaps sympathy too, is a glue that strengthens the bonds between the individual and the group. The dull routine of the back office was punctuated with exclamations like "I hate this machine!" "How can we get any work done with phones always ringing?" and "The branches still aren't filling in requisitions correctly." If the complaint was valid (more on validity in a moment), the response would take the form of laughter, a comment along the lines of "Oh, I know," "Terrible, isn't it," or a rejoinder in the form of another complaint. If not, sympathy would be withheld, and the response would be a mocking "Awwww" and laughter, a comment like "Oh, come on," or, worse, silence.

This phenomenon is not unique to back office departments. In the public space of the banking hall, exclamations are kept to a minimum, but people whisper across desks and form into small huddles to exchange complaints and condolences. In the bank vault or file room, over beers in the pub at lunch, behind the closed door of a manager's office, in the car on the way to see a customer, in conference rooms before meetings, in staff rooms while the kettle is boiling: all across the Bank, as regularly as peach, fish, and banana time in Roy's (1959–60) Clicking Department, time out from work is taken up with this ritual exchange.

VALIDITY AND LEGITIMACY

The pattern of exchange is structured by two notions: what counts as a valid complaint and what constitutes an appropriate response. Validity hinges on audience perceptions of the complainant and the opinion expressed in the complaint itself. As I have argued, derogations—distinct from deprecations—are not solicitations of redress. One does not make fun of the Bank in the expectation that someone will hear and make things better. One derogates to get a laugh, some understanding, or sympathy. But, if the derogation is to work in this way, the audience must agree with the opinion expressed by the complainant. Complaints about the weather do not work as conversation starters unless there is agreement that the weather is bad. Otherwise, the complaint is unwarranted and, thus, invalid. Further, the audience must agree that the complainant deserves (although he expresses neither desire for nor expectation of) redress. My complaint about office ergonomics would not have worked to bolster my insider status had the others not agreed that my desk was uncomfortable and that, all else equal, I deserved to be more comfortable. If redress is seen to be undeserved, the complaint is a whinge (what in American English would be called *whining*) and, thus, invalid.

Evaluations of the complaint are contingent on the relationship between complainant and audience. A joke about the Bank's technology that provokes feelings of bonhomie when voiced by an insider is an insult in other mouths, as I found to my discomfort on several occasions. With every new group in BritArm that I studied, I had to earn anew my derogation privileges. Derogation acts to reproduce and reinforce bonds between the individual and the group, but it cannot produce them where they do not exist. Certainly, an outsider cannot expect to make friends in the Bank by insulting BritArm, but merely working for BritArm does not give one carte blanche to be derogatory about the Bank either. It would be misleading to suggest that there were hard-and-fast rules as to when sympathy would be given rather than offense taken—there was much individual variation. Some people seemed to be so unpopular that they could not complain about rainy weather without being contradicted; others had the savoir faire of the court jester and could get away with almost any remark.

There are two important overarching patterns, however. The first is that derogatory remarks are more likely to elicit positive responses when their target is an aspect equally close to or equally distant from the salient contexts of the complainant and the audience. So, for example, the manager of the Securities Centre and a branch manager could joke together over lunch about the ineptitude of Head Office, the backwardness of another region, or the quirks of members of their own regional management. But a derogatory remark by the branch manager about the quality of service being provided by the newly centralized back office operations would not be found so funny or endearing.

The second pattern is that derogatory remarks are more likely to elicit sympathy and understanding when the hierarchical distance between complainant and audience is slight. Derogations among peers or between subordinate and superior are not problematic; introduce two or more layers of the hierarchy between the complainant and the audience, however, and misunderstanding is more likely. I was told by senior managers that it was inappropriate for them to share any negative feelings that they may have about the Bank or its policies with junior managers or staff, and I seldom saw this norm violated—although, often enough, those negative feelings do trickle down as senior managers share derogations with their subordinates, who might share them with their subordinates, and so on.

Equally seldom does derogation by someone low in the hierarchy elicit empathy or sympathy from someone higher up. The problem in this case is that signals break down and that derogations are taken for deprecations. As we shall see in the next section, the desire for change that distinguishes a deprecation from a derogation is not always (or even often) explicitly stated. Sometimes it is only hinted at. So long as the audience knows that they cannot be expected to provide redress for the complaint, there is no confusion. More specifically, confusion is avoided so long as the general formula of cultural sharing holds: "I know, I know that everybody else knows, and I know that everybody else knows that everybody else knows." But ambiguity can creep in if the complainant is uncertain whether his audience can offer redress or if the audience does not know whether they can reasonably be expected to.

Of course, this can happen even where there is no hierarchical distance between the complainant and the audience. A team leader who talks in a managers' meeting about the absenteeism among doers 1 will likely receive sympathy from his peers but maybe also advice on how to deal with the situation. At times, when people complained to me about the Bank, I was unsure whether they wanted my opinion, my sympathy, or my help (thinking, perhaps, that I had some influence in the organization). This caused me considerable anxiety: to offer an opinion or advice when sympathy was requested was to risk insulting the person by implying that I thought I knew better than he or she did what to do; to offer sympathy when redress was requested was to risk frustrating the person by appearing to be unwilling to help. Perhaps feeling it best always to assume that anyone complaining up the hierarchy expected redress, and, anyway, restricted by the cultural expectation of stoicism from appearing sympathetic to less senior personnel expressing negative views about the Bank, managers treated virtually all complaints (actually few in number) directed to them from down the hierarchy as deprecations.

Another reason that there are few complaints up the hierarchy is that junior people take quite a risk making a derogatory remark to a senior manager: he (and most, although not all, senior managers are men) may take it as an insult, and the consequences could be severe. Characteristically, the greater the distance between two people in the Bank hierarchy, the more likely it is that the more senior will feel it incumbent on him to act as a representative of the Bank as a whole and toe its official line, whatever his private thoughts.

The culture does, however, provide a framing (Goffman 1974, 11) within which insulting the bosses is not only feasible but mandatory: the roast. Throughout the year, but especially near the Christmas holidays, the BritArm social calendar is full of office parties, traditional breakfasts and dinners, and other official gatherings. For many of these events, a roast—a carefully prepared comedy routine consisting almost entirely of derogatory comments and inside jokes about the Bank and often focusing in particular on one person, either the most senior person present or the person in whose honor the gathering has been called (e.g., someone having a birthday or retiring)—is de rigueur. This cultural form reaches its apogee in events like the annual Regional Office Christmas pantomime, where the roast moves from the periphery to the center of the festivities. In England, a *pantomime* is a children's comic play, typically a parody of a well-known story or fairy tale, usually involving cross-dressing, and typically performed at Christmas time. Unlike at an American pantomime, neither the actors nor the members of the audience (who are encouraged to cheer, jeer, and sing along) are expected to remain silent during the performance.

The Regional Office Christmas pantomime involves hours of personal time devoted by the staff to writing the satirical script and songs, preparing outrageous costumes, and rehearsing the act. In 1994, the Christmas pantomime boasted a *Wizard of Oz* theme, where Dorothy, the Lion (he has no courage, he explains, so he couldn't get a job in Operations), the Scarecrow (with no brain, Dorothy quips, he must be from Securities Centre), and the Tin Man (with no heart, he could be from either Operations or Lending) go in search of the Vision at the end of the yellow-brick road.

Operations is picked on because, in BritArm, it is the department best known, and least loved, for overseeing the work-measurement program, which determines the "establishment," that is, the number of staff a branch or an office ought to have, a figure based on the amount of work that there is to be done. Virtually every branch and office in the Bank has more staff than its establishment, so, in making and presenting its calculations, Operations is seen as taking away staff. In fact, all it does is take away the legitimacy of current staff numbers as it has no authority to reassign or terminate employees.

The story was broken into chapters, and between each chapter came a skit performed by the various departments in Regional Office. These skits ranged from the Corporate Banking Group staging a mock television news program (replete with one-liners like "A fire in the Securities Centre caused by a cigarette butt was put out before serious good was done") to Operations singing the theme from *Oliver* ("Consider yourself downsized, consider yourself part-time, consider yourself deskilled . . .").

There were lots of inside jokes—many references in particular to a young clerk who had been caught in the act on two separate occasions the past year with two different female members of staff and to a corporate account executive (CAE) who had whinged incessantly because he had been given a red company car and he didn't like red. An extremely short operations manager was teased relentlessly about his height, as was a manager transferred in from Yorkshire about his accent and frankness ("I like what I say, and I say what I bloody well like," his caricature intoned repeatedly).

The centrality of complaint to the BritArm culture can perhaps be seen in the attention paid in events like this to transgressions of the norms of complaining. In the case of the CAE, his complaints about his car (deprecations, not derogations—he tried hard to have the color changed) were deemed whinges. In the case of the new manager from Yorkshire, he repeatedly pushed the limits, complaining too often about how things were done in this region for someone there such a short time. The stereotype of the blunt-speaking Yorkshireman offered both an explanation and a way in which to tease him about this.

The climax of the evening came at the moment of denouement, when the Wizard of Oz was revealed to be John Davidson (CEO of BritArm Group), who needed help bringing his creation, Michaelstein (a reference to Michael Cole, head of BritArm UK), to life. Michaelstein was a lifeless drone, unable to do more than endlessly repeat Michael Cole's characteristic hand gestures, until vital ingredients, including the region's own statement of aims and principles, were added to his Vision and he came to life in the requisite happy ending.

The pantomime was a mix of many different genres of derogation. It ranged from coarse jokes about the personal attributes of individuals (height, accent, sexual appetite) to subtle satire about current events in the organization (the centralized manner in which the Bank's Vision was crafted and rolled out). It was inclusive at times (departments making fun of their own stereotypes) and exclusive at others (jokes at the expense of the Securities Centre, whose management and staff were not invited). It made fun at both the individual level (the CAE and his cursed red car) and the group level (the Securities Centre, the Operations and Lending Departments). Held out of hours in a makeshift auditorium in Regional Office, with food and drinks provided at the Bank's expense, the Christmas pantomime was videotaped for posterity, and for those (Michael Cole and John Davidson included) who could not be there to see it live, and attended (and applauded) by all the senior regional management. Edward Tollerton, the regional executive director and always a reluctantly good sport about these events, noted dryly before making his way to the pantomime: "Well, I guess it is time to go down and have rude things said about me."

The event may not have been an official Bank function, but it was by no means an underground affair. This is no surprise: it is not countercultural in any sense. Because of their sharpness and their upward hierarchical trajectory, the attacks are circumscribed in a framing that sets them apart from the normal flow of activity. If one wants to make fun of management, one prepares one's lines ahead of time and always serves alcohol. The social life of the Bank, both during and outside work hours, revolves around derogation in its many forms. The pantomime is merely an exaggerated and (self-consciously low-brow) artistic form of the Brit-Arm custom of making merriment of complaint.

Deprecations

Unlike derogations, deprecations are criticisms expressing an "earnest desire that something may be averted or removed." Deprecations are antagonistic to the status quo; they are solicitations of redress. But clear, direct deprecation is rare in BritArm because it can provoke embarrassment. It can cause a loss of face by pointing out inadequacy or by forcing a public statement of unwillingness or inability to provide redress. Aversion to embarrassment is a powerful force in the Bank, and it leads to distinct patterns of deprecation, patterns that this section will examine.

It is worth pointing out first, however, that BritArm is once again reflecting broader British culture in its antipathy to embarrassment. The ready and delicate sense of what is fitting and proper in dealing with others so as to avoid giving offense or causing embarrassment is summarized in the word *tact*. Although it is by no means the case that every Brit possesses the gift of tact, it is undeniable that the British understand themselves to be a tactful people. I was made aware of this repeatedly—in the nicest possible way, naturally—during my time in the Bank. Atop the list of groups of people that the British do not consider to be particularly tactful sit the Americans. But it was not just the brute fact of my American upbringing that led me to violate norms of politeness by being too blunt, too forward, or by making explicit things better left unsaid. Fieldwork is not a tactful enterprise. Inherent in the practice are imposing oneself on others, trying to make explicit what they take for granted, asking blunt questions, and all the time writing things down in a notebook.

It is not that I was constantly seen as obnoxiously rude. Allowances can always be made for foreigners, and my status as an academic excused many strange behaviors. Also, the people in BritArm, and, indeed, the British in general, see themselves, not just as tactful, but tactful to a fault. Often, when people were nice enough to explain to me how rude I had just been, they expressed their criticism in the form of an apology for how absurdly tactful I must find the British. It was on one of these occasions that I was told the story of someone from BritArm who was on a train and noticed that there was a couple in the same carriage who were having sex. Nobody said a word, studiously ignoring the two (or at least pretending to) until they finished and lit up cigarettes. Then someone said: "Excuse me, this is a no-smoking compartment."

Whether there was a BritArm employee on the train that day is questionable, but otherwise the story is true. Here is the account from *The Times*:

Passengers on a crowded train said nothing when a couple had sexual intercourse in their second-class, no-smoking carriage, and protested only when the lovers lit up post-coital cigarettes.

John Henderson, 29, a warehouseman and Zoe D'Arcy, 19, were returning to London from a store's bank holiday day-trip to Margate when their feelings got the better of them, Nazir Afzal, for the prosecution, told Horseferry Road magistrates court, central London, yesterday.

The couple, interrupted in first-class, entered a crowded compartment packed with passengers, including children. "Miss D'Arcy got up and went to the toilet, and came out carrying her jeans and wearing only her knickers on the lower part of her body," said Mr. Afzal. "She was then seen to sit on Mr. Henderson's lap and they performed full sexual intercourse. In due course, they finished and lit up a cigarette each."

Until that point, nobody complained, said Mr. Afzal. "It was only on their action in lighting up the cigarettes that the witnesses actually came up to them and complained about their behaviour." The court heard that a guard radioed ahead to police at Victoria.

Henderson, of Pimlico, southwest London, and D'Arcy, of Hanwell, northwest London, pleaded guilty to committing an indecent act on May 25 on the train between Margate and Victoria. They also admitted lighting up a cigarette in a no-smoking carriage. They were each fined £50 and ordered to pay £25 costs. ("No Smoking Please" 1992)

The story was told to me as an example of how British tact can be stretched to the improbable length of a crowded carriage of people studiously ignoring a sex act being performed only a few feet away and in plain view. But what makes it so funny, of course, is, not just that nobody complained about this couple having sex, but that someone *did* complain about them smoking. What accounts for the distinction? First of all, some complaints are easier to make than others because they are more normal, they are rehearsed, we are used to hearing them and making them. Second, the carriage was clearly marked as no smoking in a way that it was not, for example, marked as no sex—that condition presumably being implicit. The clarity and explicitness of the smoking prohibition allows the use of British Rail rules as an intermediary to the deprecation, to depersonalize it. Perhaps afraid that other people, although pretending not to watch, were enjoying the show (in an illicit way, a reaction that secondhand smoke seldom elicits), potential complainants might fear being considered prudish and being told to mind their own business by the couple with the tacit agreement of ogling fellow passengers. With a clear rule violation, this fear is mitigated.

In BritArm, too, we find that complaints about certain things are re-hearsed and repeated often while others are never made and that, when made, complaints are often depersonalized. These patterns are both part of the larger complex cultural pattern of deprecation in the Bank that I learned in large part by clashing with it. This larger pattern and the tac-tics that generate it are provisions from broader British culture, but it is important to recognize the way in which they are adapted for use in BritArm. In this case, they are hyperbolized. People in BritArm are more British in the importance that they place on discretion and embarrass-ment avoidance than is the British public as a whole. Tact and discretion are especially prized in the Bank, it was explained to me many times, be-cause of the nature of the Bank's work: dealing with people's money and their financial problems. Never mind sex, I was told; the British public is intensely private about questions of money. Discretion must be absolute when probing a customer's financial situation. Tact is required when deny-ing a loan or dealing with customer complaints. Employees are taught this from the moment they enter the Bank, and the message is constantly reinforced.

Note that this is true of banking even in the United States—despite the stereotype widely held in Europe that Americans are obscenely will-ing to discuss money (how much we make and how much we have paid for things). Even if this relative stereotype is modally accurate, Americans do not like their bankers to talk about their money. In this sense, I doubt that much has changed since Argyris (1954, 74) found in his ethnography of an American bank a strong aversion to embarrassment among the em-ployees and a belief that "tact and diplomacy" are by far the most often required abilities in their formal work. In that bank, however, according to Argyris, this led, not to tactful deprecation, but to an absence of dep-recation. As he quotes one employee saying: "The complainers may com-plain to themselves, but they'll just sit here and take it—no matter what they get." The difference in BritArm is that it is not the complainers, com-plaining among themselves, who are the minority. The minority in Brit-Arm are those who, for one reason or another, refuse to join in the wel-coming chorus of complaint. I will examine that group in a moment.

DENIABLE DEPRECATIONS

Ambiguity is central to how the stereotypically British tactics of tact are used in the Bank. By merely hinting at, rather than clearly stating, nega-tivity and desire for change, speakers leave it up to listeners to decide whether to interpret remarks as deprecations. This can happen uninten-tionally, as when one makes a derogation only to have it interpreted as a deprecation by someone taking a hint that one did not intend to give. The comfortable exchange of complaint and condolence is disrupted in such a case by unexpected aid and advice or countercomplaint ("What do you want *me* to do about it?"). But ambiguity is commonly used on purpose to make deniable deprecations. There is embarrassment associated with having to ask (or having to be asked) for redress that one feels should have been offered. There is also embarrassment associated with requests that are refused. When presented with only a hint of request, one can offer redress without having been asked or silently refuse by treating the remark as a derogation and offering sympathy and understanding instead.

Deniable deprecations are used in the Bank to complain about everything from the coffee to career advancement. Managers would typically be served coffee each morning and tea each afternoon. Assistant managers and clerical officers, however, make their own hot drinks. Most branches and offices have a kitchen with a sink, a kettle, and a small fridge packed with pint-sized cartons of milk that people bring in for this purpose. Groups form of people who trade off making each other hot drinks. Turn taking is loosely regulated. Perceived free riding—free drinking in this case, never taking a turn at making tea for others—may be dealt with by direct deprecation, but it is more often handled through deniable deprecation.

Consider the following example. One midmorning in the Securities Centre, Helen, a doer 1 on our team, said, apparently to nobody in particular: "What time is it? I'm thirsty." She smacked her lips for effect. "Kathy, are you thirsty?" Kathy smiled and nodded. "Oi, Tom, we're thirsty," Helen said. "You're thirsty, are you?" "Mmm: parched." "I guess it's my turn to make the tea, then, is it?" "Oh, that would be nice, yes please. Coffee for me." Helen, with the collusion of Kathy, complained to Tom, without explicitly complaining, about his having forgotten that it was his turn to play mother.

These trivial pleasantries can be seen as rehearsals for more important episodes like deniably deprecating with regard to a promotion delayed. For example, a branch clerk whom I shadowed complained repeatedly to me and her colleagues that she had been promised a job upstairs some time ago but was still stuck covering the Customer Service Desk. This branch, like many, was arranged to have the entire ground floor dedicated to cashiers, the Customer Service Desk, and private interview rooms in which to talk to customers. The upstairs held the managers' offices and the desks of the assistant managers and clerks who dealt with lending and account maintenance. A job upstairs meant, in this case, not a promotion, but a chance to learn new skills and to have some variety.

Despite being very vocal to others and to me about the broken prom-ise, she said nothing in front of the branch manager except to joke from time to time about how routine the job had become since she had done it for so long. Without fail, the manager took these comments as deroga-tions and replied in kind. She just shrugged me off when I asked why she was not more explicit about her complaint. Wasn't it obvious? Her man-ager had, however, taken the hint, as I found out later in talking to him. The promise had not been forgotten. The problem, he said, was that, with staff cutbacks, the branch could not afford to lose her off the Cus-tomer Service Desk. He felt bad, but there was nothing to be done about it for the time being.

This sort of thing happens at all levels of the Bank. "Naked ambition is unseemly here," I was told. To be considered "ambitious" is to be part way toward "political" in the continuum that eventually leads from "good man" to "absolutely untrustworthy." "You Americans are different," the same manager told me. "You don't have to be embarrassed to say, 'This is my goal; this is what I want to achieve; I deserve this.' People respect that in the States, don't they? It's different here." I shrugged, as I did whenever possible in situations like that.

To create useful ambiguity, deprecations need not be made to re-semble derogations. They can also be made in the form of neutral state-ments of fact. A common complaint among human resources managers and good performers in the Bank is that managers are neither willing nor able to give sufficient negative feedback to their staff. Mediocre perfor-mance persists, they argue, because managers are too worried about sparing the feelings, and saving the faces, of their subordinates to com-plain about them to Human Resources—unless they go so far as to break a rule or violate policy.

Certainly there is a lot of individual variation in all this, but the shape of the overall pattern can perhaps be gleaned from the behavior of the outliers. I spent time shadowing two managers with reputations for al-most alarming forthrightness. Speaking of one of these men, an inform-ant told me: "He lets you know where you stand with him, and some don't like him, but I respect him for it." Yet this manager himself told me that I was naive when I observed him complaining about the performance of a subordinate to a third party and asked why he did not raise the issue with the subordinate directly. "Oh, I will," he told me, "but we're not as blunt as you Americans. You don't want to destroy his morale. You want to talk to him in a way where he understands the situation for himself, where he needs to change. Don't beat around the bush. I'll ask him how he sees the situation. He'll get the hint. And he'll know I'm watching him."

Whether the subordinate got the hint is hard for me to ascertain—I never spoke to him privately. He certainly appeared nervous in response to his manager's question of how he thought things were going.

The sometimes overly tactful way in which managers deal with subordinates is hardly surprising when we remember that most of them will have customer responsibility as well and that almost all of them will have been promoted into management positions because of their demonstrated ability to deal well with customers. They are simply treating staff in ways carefully learned for treating customers. And any deprecation of the customer must be done with the utmost tact.

I saw several times how tricky it can be to get business customers to pay the charges and fees that they owe without hurting the Bank's relationship with them. Lending managers have the discretion to waive many charges and fees if they deem it necessary to keep a good business customer from going to another bank or to attract a good customer from a competitor. Customers know this, and, consequently, many see all bank charges as negotiable. Getting the customer to pay fees was high on the agendas of many of the managerial visits to customer sites that I shadowed, but on only one occasion did a literal asking and negotiation process occur. More common was a sort of dance, with the bank manager trying to raise the issue of fees without being seen to raise it, the customer trying to refuse to pay without being seen to refuse, and the bank manager trying to insist on payment without being seen to insist.

In an amusing keying (Goffman 1974, 44), one customer interrupted an ongoing episode of such repartee with an aside to me: "He's a clever man [*nods at David Stout, the manager*]: he wants me to pay for his services, that's what this is about. And nothing comes for free. But I'm a good earner for him [*turns to David*], aren't I David? [*David agrees that he is a good customer.*] I can't let him have everything he wants [*winks at me*]." Having achieved the victory of at least partial payment, David laughed, said that they would talk about that later, and changed the subject. By speaking through me, the customer was able to start a negotiation with the manager without losing face or seeming crass while simultaneously doing David the favor of showing kindness to the researcher he had brought along.

DEPERSONALIZED DEPRECATIONS

This raises the second tactic of tactful deprecation that I want to discuss: the use of intermediaries and depersonalization. Where deprecation is clear, it is typically indirect. In part, the use of intermediaries in deprecation is due to a bureaucratic protocol of complaint in the Bank according to which one is supposed to direct most complaints to one's manager, who starts a complaint on its way through the proper channels to the appropriate party. A complaint may be heard and repeated by a half dozen people, then, before it is heard by someone who can do more about it than pass it along. Even in cases in which that protocol does not apply or is being ignored, deprecations are very often made in the Bank through intermediaries to spare the complainant and the recipient the embarrassment of having to face each other and cope with the reactions provoked.

Fears of deprecation creating embarrassing scenes seem well founded. Perhaps because of the rarity of direct deprecation, even mild rebukes can provoke passionate reactions. One day while I was sitting with Cutler learning the ways of the doer 2, his colleague, Joan, took a call from a corporate account executive about a planning report on some land he was proposing the Bank take to secure a loan. The manager told Joan that Cutler had promised last week to look into prices for the report and order it; now he was calling to check what progress had been made. None. Cutler says that he remembers talking to the guy but that he never promised to get a report and would never have said that he would check around about prices. That is just not something he does: the price of reports is not something that the Centre worries about, he argues. Joan tells the manager that nothing has been done yet but that they will send for the planning report right away. She tells Cutler that the manager did not sound happy as he hung up, and she goes to fax a request to a firm to do the report. Cutler is flushed and clearly upset. He repeats to Joan that he would never promise something like that, to check the prices. He tells me that complaints such as these are "really not on": "We're all one company!"

A little while later, Nick, the team leader, comes over, having just received a call from the manager to complain. Cutler says that he honestly doesn't remember what he said to the manager but that he doesn't think that he promised to price and obtain the report. Nick tells him not to worry, that they are all under a lot of pressure and have so many things going on at once that it is no wonder they might forget one or two. He quickly adds that he's not saying that Cutler *did* forget to send the report. Cutler explains to me that it seems he may have screwed up. He repeats that he can't recall exactly what happened. They just get too many calls. These people in the branches, he says, think that the Centre is here working only for them. But they have dozens of branches to serve.

Nick gets off the phone and asks to speak to Cutler. He says that he told the manager essentially not to worry about the planning report because it is a postreliability formality. This means that it is Bank policy to release the loan funds to the customer before this formality is completed. The manager, Nick says, gave him grief about this, saying that, if that is true, it shouldn't be. After all, if we find out afterward that there is a motorway about to be built through the land, we would really be stuck. Cutler goes to the small bookcase of loose-leaf binders containing action sheets and selects the appropriate volume. It is not clear from the action sheets, however, whether checking the planning report is a pre- or postreliability formality. The computer system indicates that it is postreliability, but, to double-check, Cutler goes back to the progress sheets that the Bank used before the process was semiautomated. To his relief, it confirms the postreliability status of planning reports.

Cutler and Nick talk about it some more, however, and Nick says that the manager has a point with his motorway example and suggests that Cutler call the Legal, Technical, and Securities Department (LT&S) in London to clarify the issue and find out why this formality is postreliability. Also, he suggests that Cutler call the firm handling the report to see whether it can be handled as a rush job. While on hold with LT&S, Cutler asks Ken, a doer 2 on another team, what he thinks. Ken says that planning reports almost never turn up anything and that they can take months to get. LT&S confirms this analysis and notes that, if the manager is concerned, he has the discretion to hold the money back until the report is obtained.

Cutler complains to me that this manager is being difficult about this because he thinks that he was promised a planning report. He is just causing trouble about this reliability issue because he is annoyed with the Securities Centre. Hearing this, Nick tells Cutler that the manager was not angry with him and seemed quite decent about the whole thing. Cutler is mollified by that and goes back to work, having spent over an hour on this issue. There is no telling how differently this episode would have gone had the complaint been made directly to Cutler and not to Joan and then Nick. The interesting thing is that putting the two parties directly concerned on the phone together was never even suggested.

Even if intermediaries have not been used to mitigate embarrassment in the first place, they can still be used to repair its effects afterward. Sometimes this is done without the knowledge of the complainant. For example, Walter—an elderly assistant manager at the Securities Centre considered abrasive but technically impeccable, largely because he had been doing nothing but securities work for ten years or more—called a CAE to point out a mistake in a piece of security that the manager had taken for one of his customer's loans. The manager said that he didn't care. Walter expressed surprise at this, and the conversation grew a little heated as Walter told the manager that he ought to care, that this was the sort of information that the manager needed to make a lending decision. The manager angrily asked Walter not to tell him how to do his job. Walter said, "I bid you good afternoon, sir!" and hung up on the manager. Despite often complaining themselves that Walter is "a bit of a dick," the other clerks rallied around him now with the sentiment "Right on, Wal-ter: you tell him." They laughed with him and said that his old-fashioned language—"I bid you good afternoon, sir!"—was wonderful.

A short time later, Cutler got a call from Betty, an acquaintance and the manager's personal assistant (PA). They laughed together about the incident and told each other what they had heard about what happened. Cutler admitted to Betty that he himself often complains about Walter but advised her that Walter is the sort of person who really needs to be apologized to since he will not let something like this drop. Maybe an hour later, Walter came down to say that he must carry some weight be-cause he's had Betty, the manager's PA, on the phone to apologize. Cut-ler and Nick smiled and noted dryly that Walter must have put the fear of God in them over there. In this case, the truth of the situation was kept from Walter. More often, however, the network of PAs is used explicitly by managers for this reparation purpose, as when a manager newly pro-moted to supervise his peers had his PA call the other PAs after the first area meeting to make sure that nothing he had said had been taken the wrong way.

It is much less embarrassing to face someone as an intermediary to a deprecation than as its instigator. The least embarrassing deprecations of all are those that are not instigated by any one person, those where every-one is an intermediary. This is the case when the deprecation is deper-sonalized. The deprecation's solicitation of redress is expressed as stem-ming, not from any personal desire of the complainant, but from the impersonal requirements of Bank policy. This is why, for example, per-formance problems that involve violations of policy (even minor viola-tions) are deprecated more often than those that do not, even if the prob-lems are serious. Managers rely on the much-derogated black-and-white bureaucratic inflexibility of the reams of policy action sheets to ease the derogation that is part of their job. Note that this is exactly the same find-ing made by Smith (1990, 74) in her study of an American bank. There, middle managers protested the removal of bureaucratic standards for performance evaluation. They argued that being given more flexibility would make their jobs more difficult and trouble the relationships they had with their people.

The second role of intermediaries in tactful deprecation—helping patch up relationships following a direct deprecation—can also be deper-sonalized. For example, faced with accusations of sloth and incompetence by lending managers, the Securities Centre's team leaders started inviting the assistants of these managers for half-day visits to the Centre and lunch. I knew several of those assistants, and they all came away with a higher re-gard for the team leaders and doers 2 they met, but no fewer complaints about the performance of the Centre. "They're good people, and they're working hard," one said, "but the teams have too much to do, they are understaffed, and the technology falls down. Typical BritArm, really."

This pattern is repeated time and again in the Bank. To give just one other example: complaints about information technology people who are "second-rate" and "have no clue about what we do here" morph into complaints about the system of prioritizing information technology projects and allocating time and resources to them when those information technology people are met. The shift of focus away from individuals and to "the Bank," "the system," or ongoing cost-cutting efforts is a dialectical move, merging the contradictory opinions of complainant and defendant into the higher truth of the Bank being at fault. Embarrassing deprecations are, thus, transformed into comforting diagnoses and accompanying derogations. Rather than being separated by complaints and accusations, all parties come together in shared suffering of the Bank's inadequacies. And, because *the Bank* is a fungible placeholder for everything outside the shared contexts of the speakers, this move is available to any dyad of individuals in the organization.

THE STIGMA OF BEING A COMPLAINER

A final point about deprecations. As we have seen, individuals within the Bank vary in their aversion to embarrassment. Embarrassment is not the only deterrent to inappropriate or excessive deprecation, however: there is also the stigma of being considered a complainer. A complainer is "not on board" and "not a team player"—attributes no (secretly) ambitious organization man or woman can afford to acquire. Derogation and deprecation are a regular part of the BritArm day, but, in an organization in which psychometric tests are performed to evaluate executives' enthusiasm for the Bank's Vision, knowing where to draw the line is important. "I speak my mind too much to get on in this Bank," another manager with a reputation for blunt speaking told me. "Actually, I never thought I'd get as far as I have. I won't get further."

A common complaint in the Bank—and one more common the higher you go in the hierarchy—is that there is too much complaining in the Bank. This is well-known, and, even when complaint is invited by a senior figure, reservation is warranted. Similar reservations apply to going on the record with a complaint. A small example comes from an interview with an employee published in BritArm's newsletter *Bankground* (April 1994). When the employee was asked to describe his greatest frustration in his job, he replied: "If I had to point to any frustrations, I suppose I would say working for a very large organization sometimes brings constraints which are, perhaps, necessary."

Take as a more detailed example the roundtable lunches held by George Barber, a senior executive, in a tour of the Bank designed to allow him to get out of Head Office in London and meet with "real people" to talk with them about their concerns. In the region that I was then observing, twelve members of management and staff (plus me) were invited to come and have a three-course lunch at Regional Office, to meet Barber and share their thoughts with him. I knew several people around the table and knew that they had strong feelings about several current human resource policies. But it took a concerted effort from Barber to pull the conversation away from the banalities of how nice the lunch was to the concerns that he wanted to hear about. Barber, a recent hire from outside the Bank, was a very senior figure, much higher in the BritArm hierarchy than anyone else in the room. "Who will start?" he finally demanded. Mike Archer, a regional function head, said that he would. He noted that there was a perception among some staff, fair or not, that technology is brought in imperfectly and that staff are moved out before the technology designed to replace them has proved itself. A couple of people expressed agreement and gave examples from their own units where staff shortages had led to undesirable outcomes such as branch managers having to stand in as cashiers.

Harry Evans, another regional function head, then mentioned a situation where the Securities Centre was in desperate need of people and he personally knew of twelve people in local branches who could fill those spots but could not be released by their branches because the branches could not get the junior people they needed and, thus, had to hang on to these more experienced people. Barber asked why this was. Dennis Caviar, a regional human resources manager, replied that it was because of the recruitment ban that was on at the moment. Only graduates or people recruited directly into the field sales force could be hired. Barber nodded and said that, clearly, something needed to be done. Although we obviously can't give managers carte blanche over staffing, he said, we need to be flexible.

The conversation around the table began to warm up. "The trouble is," a branch clerk said, "that staff who retire or go on maternity leave or resign or whatever aren't being replaced because one day soon it is hoped that they won't be needed because of technology or whatever. That one day seems a long time away to those people who are trying to manage now." This led to quite a bit of animated discussion about staffing levels. Barber was silent through this discussion but finally put up his hand to halt the conversation and said: "Clearly, there are a lot of things in the Bank that need improving; we all know that. But it can't be all bad. Can we hear about some good things?" An assistant manager just back from

being on secondment with a local government organization[11] volun-
teered that one need only work outside the Bank for a while to see just
how well paid and how well looked after BritArm staff are. Silence followed. After a moment, Pete McLeod, a chief manager responsible for
ten branches and a man known for his forthrightness, commented that he
thought that it was healthy to talk openly about the bad things in the
Bank: it helped identify areas where improvement was needed. Archer,
seeming to regret having opened his mouth earlier, said that he agreed
with Barber that people in BritArm are too negative. A discussion ensued
about how overly negative people in the Bank are.

Barber then asked how morale was. Caviar said that he had been on
many branch visits and that he always asked that question and was always
told that morale in the unit in question was high but that across the bank it
was low. He said that he attributed that fact to people identifying strongly
with their unit and feeling appreciated by their unit but not by the rest of
the bank. McLeod said that he was not sure about the word *morale* but that
he thought that, in this region, it was pretty good. He said that this lunch
showed that this region is different than most, more open. Sarah, an assistant manager, agreed that it was like night and day, the difference between this region and the region where she started in the Bank. In that
region, she said, people would never be this open. "And [your old region]
is a good region, Sarah," said Archer, "so is it really better this way?" "It
is better for me," Sarah said, looking at Barber, who smiled at her.

Barber closed the meeting soon afterward by thanking everyone for
coming. Playing the comfortable role of intermediary, he said: "I'll pass
along the ideas I've heard today, also the ideas I've heard about staff levels, when I get the opportunity. I will get the opportunity, so they will be
passed on, but whether anything will change is another matter." Indeed,
given the norms of tactful deprecation, whether complaints provoke
change is always quite another matter.

Accounts

Accounts, as Lyman and Scott (1970, 112) put it, bridge the gap between
action and expectation. They are "explanations of unanticipated or untoward behavior." Unlike criticisms, which draw attention to the untoward behavior, accounts, when honored, deflect attention away from it.

11. Secondment is a common form of corporate community service in the United Kingdom. It is essentially an in-kind donation of an employee to a nonprofit organization. In this
case, the Bank paid this assistant manager's salary for a year while he worked for the local government organization.

Unlike diagnoses, which analyze the problem situation in an effort to determine what caused it, accounts smooth over the situation in an effort to make it seem less problematic. Lyman and Scott (1970, 113–20) suggest that accounts perform these functions in one of two ways: either as *excuses*, which admit that something is wrong but deny responsibility, or as *justifications*, which accept responsibility for something but deny the pejorative quality of it. In drawing this distinction, they are building on the work of Austin (1961, 124), and, as Benoit (1995) argues in his recent review of the literature, their conceptualization has over the past 30 years proved itself to be robust and useful.

The interesting thing about accounts in BritArm is that good news is as likely as bad news to be unanticipated or untoward and require explaining. The most striking example of this is the accounting described in chapter 2 given to excuse the Bank's financial results. More mundane, and more common, examples are the accounts given for why, if the Bank is as boring and as bad a place to work as it is made out to be, people nevertheless take jobs and continue to work there. Jackall's (1978) findings offer an interesting comparison here since central to his ethnographic study of an American bank are the ways in which clerks excuse and justify working for the bank. Jackall argues that, "to a great extent, the everyday work experiences of bank workers are negative or, at best, neutral" (24). He describes the work of clerks as tedious and underpaid; standardized and, thus, offering no room for creativity or personal growth; fragmented and compartmentalized, leaving clerks "only with their insubstantial work and with the sense of a lack of accomplishment which that seems to foster" (164); and so stressful and exhausting that staff go home crying because of the pressure (see generally 16–41). He claims that, because of this, there is a "quiet, undramatic crisis" (24) in the people he studied: their work itself does not provide legitimating motives for doing it.

For Jackall (1978), who assumes that conflict is the natural state of society (19), the fact that this "quiet crisis" does not lead to unrest or even much complaint needs explaining. He finds the explanation in the legitimating accounts that clerks give about their work. These accounts "help actors shape a truce with their problematic situations" (59). The clerks excuse their work situation by noting, variously, that they never aspired to work for the bank but rather drifted into the job (79), that they are stuck in the bank because they have been taught few marketable skills (80), that they will not put up with it much longer (37), that they may be changing jobs in the bank soon (28, 43). They justify their jobs by arguing, variously, that any other job they could get would be as bad as the one they have now (36), that their job is better than some other jobs they know of (38,

116), that the deprivations that they face are made up for by the security that they receive (88), and that their work is a relatively unimportant part of their lives compared to their free-time activities (163).

I found the situation in BritArm to be richer and less one-dimensional than that described by Jackall. I heard accounts similar to those that Jackall heard—and others that he did not—when talking to employees of BritArm. And, like Jackall, I found that many people in the Bank seemed to feel that their jobs lacked sufficient legitimate intrinsic or extrinsic motivation. They felt the need to excuse or justify their work situations to me in our conversations. But, significantly, I never overheard them giving such accounts of themselves to one another. The accounts were ready to hand and seemed well rehearsed, but they were voiced only when provoked by my questions. This is not an area where accounting is required in the Bank. Unlike ethnographers or other outsiders, colleagues do not ask—either explicitly or implicitly—of one another, "If things are as bad as you say, why do you stay?" For a Bank insider, unlike for an outsider, constantly complaining about a job that one has no intention of leaving is not "unanticipated or untoward behavior." It is a normal part of life in an unpopular culture.

Jackall does not make it clear whether the accounts that he describes were always the result of his prompting or whether they were voiced spontaneously. They may have been spontaneous. Voluntary turnover, low in BritArm, was high in the bank that Jackall studied (Jackall 1978, 81). With people commonly leaving, there may have been a cultural need for those staying to excuse or justify themselves to each other. What is more, the picture drawn by Jackall of the bank that he studied is more uniformly bleak than what I observed in BritArm. Although I recognize in BritArm the tedium, standardization, fragmentation, and poor remuneration that he describes, I also found warmth, humor, and camaraderie. I found people making tedious work more fun by endlessly making fun of it. Whereas Jackall found staff avoiding each other to sit at different tables in the lunch room, I found people going to the pub together for lunch. Whereas Jackall found people enduring miserable jobs in silence, I found people derogating as miserable jobs that they admitted sometimes enjoying ("I know it sounds crazy, but I actually enjoy securities," a Securities Centre team leader told me, glancing over his shoulder conspiratorially to make sure that we were not being overheard).

Nevertheless, employees keep excuses and justifications for working in the Bank well rehearsed because they are occasionally needed outside BritArm. As I noted earlier, BritArm, along with the other major clearing banks in Britain, has a poor public image, and the stereotype of bank work is not favorable in most social circles. For many employees, as Jackall puts it, "their job is a source of occasional status deprivation in their social sphere" (Jackall 1978, 103). Working for the Bank can sometimes be an embarrassment, a discredit to the employee's self-image. Excuses and justifications help bridge the gap between one's view of self and society's occupational stereotype. Lyman and Scott (1970, 128) argue that organizations systematically provide such accounts for their members. But my study suggests that the organization need not be the primary provider. With few exceptions, the excuses and justifications that employees give for working in the Bank are either generic to the occupation of banking or tied to particular subgroups and subcultures within the Bank.

I ONLY WORK HERE

First there are explanations along the lines of "I only work here." This includes both the excuse that the person drifted into the Bank without any real idea of wanting to become a banker and the justification that it does not matter what the job is like because work comes second to family, hobbies, or other activities outside the Bank. The stereotype about bankers is true for those who embrace the role, this account confirms, but that does not include me. If not bankers, then what are they? Just employees. Unlike the stereotypical Los Angeles waiter who is "really" an actor, the outside interest invoked in these accounts is seldom another career. It is more likely a recreational sport or travel.

An interesting keying of this type of account came in a manager's meeting that I observed in a medium-sized branch. Paul Lemon, the branch manager, said in the meeting that it had become clear in his VIP on Friday (his Valuing Individual Performance review with his boss) that the Bank's attitude toward staff is now to be "If you want to only work nine to five, then go do it somewhere else." He asked Richard, the head cashier, what he thought about that. Richard said that people downstairs (meaning the cashiers and the people who man the Customer Service Desk) have a nine-to-five mentality that will be tough to change. Paul said that he understands their attitudes and sympathizes. He only really became interested in banking at age twenty-eight (ten years or so after he joined the Bank). Before that, it was just a nine-to-five job for him to put some money in his pocket to spend on what he was really interested in. This gets a laugh and starts a guessing game about what he might have really been interested in.

Twenty-year-old Richard was, Paul told me privately, bright and capable but not particularly earnest or dedicated. He had a nine-to-five mentality and worked mainly to finance his various trips around the country to watch the area's football (soccer) team play. Paul was not just talking about himself in the meeting; he was talking about Richard. He was giving Richard both a warning and an honorable way to account for the change in attitude and behavior that he was suggesting. Whether Richard accepted either is hard to say. When I later spent time with Richard, learning the ways of a head cashier, I asked him how he liked his job. "It's all right," he replied. "Do you like football?" And he would be drawn no further on his feelings about the job.

I AM STUCK HERE

A second group of accounts has the theme "I am stuck here." An example comes from one of the team leaders in the Securities Centre. After observing him spend a long day doing little else besides checking in detail every aspect of all the security perfected by the members of his team, as Bank policy requires, I asked him why he stays with the Bank when he finds the work so tedious. His reply: "Where else would I go? [*Laughs.*] My skills are all in banking. If I left banking, I'd have to start all over again, and I don't want that. And there's no point going to another bank. They're all more or less the same as us, and most aren't hiring anyway." He combines the excuse that his skills are not transferable, except to another bank, with the justification that all banks are the same to arrive at the conclusion that there is no point leaving for the competition.

The belief that the competition is no different from BritArm is shared in (possibly apocryphal) stories like the following. David Stout, a chief manager, had been a Bank inspector for a while and told me that there were lots of stories about inspectors but that his favorite was about a senior guy who really liked his drink quite a bit and after lunch one day went into a branch for a routine inspection. David said: "You know, all the inspectors tend to look alike, and the branches tend to look alike, and the first thing you do, the first thing any of the inspectors would do, is to ask for the keys and count the money in the till and do a check that way. So the guy got halfway through counting when he realized that he was in [one of BritArm's competitors'] branch! So he got up at that point, gave the keys back, and told them, 'Well, it was just a quick cursory spot inspection,' and walked out." I heard two other variations of the same story but could find no one who could vouch for its veracity—it has become something of a Bank myth.

THINGS COULD BE WORSE

A third theme in accounts is "Things could be worse." These are accounts that justify a particular job by comparing it to other jobs that are worse. Sometimes these other jobs are also inside the Bank. People in branches, for example, justified their jobs by comparing them to the drudgery of a Service Centre, where all one does is move paper from one side of the desk to the other. Designed like Securities Centres, with similar goals of scale efficiencies in mind, Service Centres handled telephone calls from customers, data entry, check processing, and other back office functions for a number of branches. For their part, people in the Service Centre justified their jobs by comparing them to the stresses of the Branch. One clerk at the Service Centre, for example, was very shy about having me sit with her to learn about her job: "Are you sure? You'll be so bored." I demurred, and she pulled up a chair for me. After a little while of her explaining what she did, I asked her how she liked the job. "Its OK, I guess," she said, noncommittally. "Well, you know, it does get very samey," she added after a moment, referring to the fact that it involves doing the same thing—checking customer addresses—over and over again. "But you don't mind?" I asked after sixty seconds of silence. "No. Well, I mean, I like it better than being in a branch." "Why is that?" I asked. "Oh, it's much better here." "Why?" "Well, you don't have to meet with the customers," she said. "So you can just sit down and get your job done. That's what I like most about it." She picked up her neatly printed list of customer accounts and carefully put a tick by the customer whose address she had just checked.

Other times, however, the comparison is with jobs and careers outside the Bank, a manager (always a manager, never anyone lower in grade) carrying on with a number of derogations about the Bank but then telling me that I had to put the complaints in the context of how grateful he was to the Bank. For example, a business manager told me: "This place has problems." In fact, he had just spent the better part of a day telling me of them. "But I want to finish my career here, and if that means staying in this job until I retire, then so be it. Does that surprise you?" I shrugged. "I owe a lot to BritArm. I've only got three O-levels," he said, meaning that he had left school at sixteen. He stared at me to gauge my reaction. "My father was a miner. And now I'm a bloody fucking bank manager. [*Laughs.*] I'm meeting with company directors and such like. So when I complain about my job, understand that the Bank has given me more than I had a right to expect."

Unlike other accounts, this one was particular to BritArm as an organization. Some of BritArm's High Street competitors are "public school banks."[12] BritArm, on the other hand, was a "state school bank": the implication is that breeding was not necessary to get ahead in

12. In England, *public schools* are elite, private schools. Eton and Harrow are the two most famous public schools for boys. The nearest American equivalent might be expensive, private boarding schools such as Choate, Exeter, or Phillips Andover. *State schools* are what are called *public schools* in the United States.

BritArm. This willingness of the organization to overlook one's lowly background excused much for some managers.

I AM THE STEREOTYPICAL BANKER

A fourth cluster of accounts concerns the security that a bank job offers. These accounts explain working for the Bank by saying "I am the stereotypical banker." The stereotypical banker in Britain prizes security above advancement, fame, or fortune. He values comforting routine over challenge or change. He prefers the safety of being told what to do to the risk of thinking for himself. He is tactful and discreet, cautious and careful. By far the most common account I heard for why people worked in the Bank involved job security—BritArm offered jobs for life—and the knowledge that, if one kept his nose clean, he would gradually advance through the ranks and likely end up a manager one day.

Job security was sometimes offered as a justification—"the work isn't so bad; after all, it is secure." But as the Bank's official line became less paternalistic—jobs were no longer going to be for life; there were going to be fewer management positions on offer; layoffs and branch closures were almost certainly going to happen—this account was more often used as an excuse. For example, a branch assistant manager said: "I joined the Bank because it was good, secure work. A job for life, right? But now there's an excess of assistant managers across the Bank. There aren't enough management jobs for those that deserve them. In the '80s, you saw people rocketing up the career ladder. Not now. I mean, I'm not an impatient man, but I don't want to be doing this [*points at his desk to indicate his current job*] forever." Because of broken promises, the security that the Bank offers is no longer a valid excuse for working there. Another account must be offered as well: usually either a denial of prolonged acceptance, as in the example given above, or something from the "I am stuck here" category.

I AM NOT THE STEREOTYPICAL BANKER

The opposite account, "I am not the stereotypical banker," also has currency in BritArm. This account works by invoking an "us," people who care about their work, about serving the customer, and about being successful, in comparison with a "them," people who care only about a secure job, a comfortable routine, and an easy life. "There are a lot of good people in the Bank," I was reminded regularly, as if that would not otherwise be obvious to me. As one young manager's assistant told me: "I don't mind putting in the extra hours. I like to be able to do things right, and I'm learning a lot. There are a number of us who typically stay late. Most of them don't give a toss. After five o'clock, they don't want to know.

I mean, of course. They joined the Bank because it was a job for life and all that. But there are some very smart people in this Bank, you know." References to the smart people in the Bank can be seen as a tactful way of suggesting that one is oneself a smart person, but, more than that, the presence of other talented people helps someone who perceives himself to be talented justify working for the Bank. I most often heard this sort of account from young senior clerical officers, assistant managers, and managers (people in their twenties and thirties). Unlike other accounts, I *overheard* this one as well as heard it as these young hard workers talked to each other about what long hours they put in and affirmed that they were all part of the same clique.

In a similar vein, a distinction between "us" and "them" is used to account for the fact that, in many parts of the Bank, local conditions seem better than the derogations would have one believe. Accounts are needed to reconcile this fact without invalidating the derogations. "It's different here," I was told in many parts of the Bank. "This region is more open." "Our manager here in the branch isn't like the rest; he doesn't play the Bank's political games." "Edward [the regional executive director] shields us from all the shit Head Office tries to dump on us and lets us get on with it." "It's different around here; people are more friendly and care about doing things right." "This office is special because of the way it was created; it has a different atmosphere than other places in the Bank." And so on. Perhaps more clearly than any other form of lay ethnography in the Bank, these culturally provided accounts about the organizational culture and the types of people within it help people work for such an unpopular organization.

Having reconciled themselves to working—and, in some cases, to working hard—for an organization deserving of the derogations heaped on it, employees are left with a potent, catchall account for a wide range of untoward events and behavior: "You know the Bank." And you also know the typical people who work for the Bank. These accounts are effortlessly used to explain everything from the weakness of the Bank's technology to its lack of entrepreneurial spirit. When one manager with whom I spoke found out that I was a management studies student, he told me up front that he did not believe in management theories like empowerment. I asked him why not. "Empowerment won't work in the Bank. Why? Because these guys want to be told what to do. These are the sort of the people who join the Bank."

Sometimes, as in the case of technology, accounts blur with derogation. Ben's derogating joke reported at the beginning of this chapter was a parody of an account, supposedly excusing the poorly designed window with reference to shared knowledge about what happens when BritArm does technology. On the other hand, the story (which I heard often) about how the Bank came to have its much-derided computer system, called ISS, is usually presented as an account but is claimed to be a derogation by some. ISS, I was told over and over, was obsolete the day it went on-line. Apparently, the company that wrote the software marketed it to all the major banks in Britain. All the other banks had the sense to reject it, but not BritArm. People familiar with the ISS project reject that account, claiming that it is a Bank myth. "Typical of people in the Bank to believe the worst," one information technology manager told me—accounting for that account. Part of what lay ethnography is called on to explain is the lay ethnography heard elsewhere in the Bank.

Diagnoses

Diagnoses are like accounts in that they are explanations of unantici-pated or untoward actions and events. Unlike accounts, however, diag-noses express antagonism, rather than acquiescence, toward the prob-lem. Diagnoses are explanations of what is wrong, of what caused, or is causing, the problem. Often, but not always, they are also accompanied by prescriptions of what ought to be done to redress the situation. To the extent that those prescriptions seem undesirable (e.g., because of pre-dicted side effects) or impossible to implement (e.g., because of the im-plied change to the culture), diagnoses blur with accounts. To the extent that descriptions of causes are seen as affixations of blame, diagnoses blur with deprecations—a common occurrence. Whenever diagnosis goes beyond self-criticism, there is the possibility of it being intended, or re-ceived, as blame shifting. As one senior executive of the Bank memorably wrote: "A common tenet of recurrent culture, as substantiated by ques-tionnaire work, is that whilst managers understand and can rationalize the need for change both in the work and personal context, that change is seen largely to be impacting upon everyone other than themselves."

In the bank that she studied, Smith (1990) found strategic management diagnosing the bank's problems as being the fault of middle management and middle management diagnosing them as being the fault of strategic management. What I found in BritArm is that it is not just top manage-ment faulting middle management and vice versa; it is everyone faulting everyone else.

When I look back over my interview notes, I see older employees fault-ing younger employees:

The problem with the Bank is that decisions are being made by Head Office boys who have never run their own unit, most of them, who do

not even have lending experience, many of them, and who have not experienced a full business cycle. So when good times come, we are told
to open the spigot and grow the lending book at all costs. And when, as
they always do, bad times come, they panic and shut off the tap. They
don't know, or care, what we've tried in the past, what has worked and
what hasn't. So we lurch from this direction to that and back again.

And I see younger employees faulting older ones:

> The trouble is that there is too much deadwood and too many old dogs
> left in the Bank. Most of the younger managers want to make the
> changes, want to make the Bank First Choice.[13] But there are a lot of
> old dogs who don't want to learn new tricks, who resist the changes,
> who put up obstacles and keep things from happening.

I see planners faulting implementation designers. As Ted Grant, a manager in Network Strategy and Development (NS&D)—the Head Office
department responsible for creating elaborate implementation plans for
strategies devised elsewhere in the Bank—explained to me:

> At Head Office they operate in a mode of what I call *reasoned failure*. Af-
> ter a few years, they know that none of these plans they so carefully
> make ever work. Now if you go talk to them, they will give you plenty
> of reasons why this is—none of which have to do with the ideas, but
> rather with the way they are implemented.

I see implementation designers, in turn, faulting implementers. As Doug
Thomas, one of the NS&D managers responsible for the implementation
design of Securities Centres (contained in a four-hundred-page implementation handbook given to each Centre manager), put it:

> The trouble with Securities Centres is that people don't follow the
> recipe. It is like baking a fruitcake—and you can take this metaphor as
> far as you like. You don't want crap fruit, but you don't need the best
> fruit either—that is like the staff. If the recipe says cook it for two hours
> at one hundred degrees, that is what you should do. You can't—like
> some regions wanted to—cook it for one hour at two hundred degrees.
> The Centres that have done best are those that have followed the recipe
> closest. Of course you can't follow it blindly, but you can follow it. The
> trouble was, I didn't have any power to force them to follow it. Very
> frustrating.

13. *First Choice* refers here to the Bank's official Vision: "To be First Choice for customers, investors, and staff." Informally, it was a code—to say that someone wanted to make the Bank First
Choice was to say that he or she was not cynical about the Vision or the change programs associated with it.

And I see implementers returning the favor and faulting implementation designers. As a member of the management team at the Securities Centre told me:

> Literally, the only parts of this Centre that are working well are those parts where we ignored the implementation handbook. It isn't realistic, it assumes a best-case world, and we would have been better off starting from scratch on our own without it.

DIAGNOSING THE SECURITIES CENTRE

The Securities Centre example illustrates well several of the patterns of diagnosis that I observed in the Bank and is, therefore, worth discussing in some detail. The Securities Centre that I studied opened in July 1993, one year before I began my fieldwork there. One of sixteen such Centres across the bank, it perfected the security for 248 branches. Its 124 employees handled approximately eleven hundred new items of security each month and worked to complete approximately eight thousand left-over items of security that had been only partially completed by branches when the Centre opened and securities work was transferred to it. Besides the manager, there were three senior assistant managers and eight assistant managers who led the eight teams of doers 1 and 2. The Centre reflected a change in practice, not only in the centralization of securities work, but also in the introduction of a computer system, TecSec, that was meant to deskill the securities perfection process and allow it to be done by less senior clerical staff than had been required before. By 1994, this Securities Centre was producing quality security—a Bank inspection found that "the standard of completion of security by the Securities Centre is particularly good"—but it was over budget by £425,000 per annum. This cost overrun came primarily from the need to have thirty-five more employees working in the Centre than had been envisioned when the budget was drawn up, and it represented 97 percent of the £440,000 that (according to the original business plan) the Bank was to have saved each year by perfecting security in a centralized unit instead of having each branch do it individually.

Further, lending managers complained that security was taking too long to be completed, thus impairing their ability to deliver customer service. There were two sorts of delays in the Securities Centre that frustrated lending managers: delays in getting the "charge form" prepared so that the customer could sign it and delays in getting the security "reliable," that is, perfected enough that it was considered safe to distribute money to the customer against it. Until the charge form was signed, the customer might well decide to borrow from another bank. If the money was disbursed late, the customer might well decide to borrow from another bank next time. The delays were sometimes so bad that managers lent money even before the security was considered safe. Ironically, then, even though the security taken was checked more thoroughly than it had been before the creation of the Centre, the Bank's security exposure was possibly greater.

The various diagnoses of the Centre's problems read like laundry lists of organizational afflictions. Cribbing from one internal Bank report, the provenance of which I discuss below, the problems with the Centre include the following:

> The Centre *manager* is weak and ineffectual. He lacks the required competencies (as described in the Implementation Handbook) for the job. His decisions to continue increasing the number of branches "taken on" by the Centre despite its troubles and to take over responsibility for partially completed security were wrongheaded.

> The *information technology,* both hardware and software, is inadequate. Hardware breakdowns lead to delays. The software requires more securities expertise to operate than was expected and its inflexibility frustrates knowledgeable users and makes it difficult for them to use their judgment to take shortcuts and expedite things.

> The *culture* of the Centre is one of "Quality of Product" rather than "Customer Service." Centre staff seem more sympathetic to the views of Group Audit than the branches and Corporate Business Groups that are their customers.

> *Human resource* difficulties and a hiring freeze have forced the Centre to operate with fewer staff than its "establishment"—i.e., the number of staff which the Regional Operations Department has determined that the Centre requires to perform its function. By 1994, this establishment figure was substantially higher than the figure used for the original business case and budgeting. It has also had to rely on fixed contract and temporary staff who have no previous experience in the Bank, who have no intuitive understanding of security matters, and who have taken longer to become proficient in their jobs than was anticipated.

> Team leaders are having to spend longer than expected checking the work of their team members and have *too little time* to manage their teams.

> At least 50% of Security Requisition forms sent to the Centre by *lending managers* are incorrectly or incompletely filled in. The Centre must

therefore contact the manager or his clerk to obtain additional information before perfection can begin.

New *Bank policy* regarding the necessity of having customers either seek independent legal advice or formally decline to do so before signing mortgage or guarantee agreements with the Bank has introduced a cumbersome and time-consuming step into the perfection process.

As befits a situation in which costs are not being saved and the Bank's exposure to risk is not being reduced while customer service is getting worse, this is a hard-hitting diagnosis. It implicates a lot of groups in the Bank—the Centre's manager and staff, lending managers, Regional Human Resources, UK Human Resources (which was responsible for the hiring freeze), Information Technology, NS&D, Regional Operations (which crafted the original business plan), Legal and Technical Services (which was responsible for the independent legal advice policy change), and others. The full report provides supporting evidence for each of its assertions and makes recommendations for resolving each perceived problem at both the local and the national levels.

Immensely frustrating to the credit risk manager, who spent weeks compiling data and conducting interviews to write the report, the diagnosis had no impact—it changed nothing in the organization. Indeed, as we shall see, it did more to reaffirm existing beliefs than to change minds, and it served more as an alibi for inaction than as a prompt for change. The ways in which the report was received and the interpretive work that was done to disarm it reveal much about the considerable cultural competence required to craft a diagnosis that will have influence in BritArm. Merely being on the right side of undisputed facts is not enough. Indeed, I never heard a single denial of any of the points made in the report. The report was not so much disbelieved as *disarmed*. People did not disagree with the items it raised, but they downplayed some items, justified or excused others, and conveniently saw in the remaining items evidence supporting whatever narrower diagnoses they already believed.

The Centre's *manager*, for example, said that he never claimed that he was a genius but that, had he been given the staff and the information technology that he had been promised, there would not have been such problems. He justified the decision to take over responsibility for partially completed items as having made good sense at the time. The decision to continue taking on branches whatever the cost he excused as being required by the "Ronald Smith directive." Ronald Smith was the Bank's customer service director. This "directive," as it was always referred to, was a memo sent to all Securities Centres expressing Smith's desire and expectation that all branches in all Centres be taken on by the end of

1994. For his part, Smith denied that his memo was meant as a directive; he claimed that he meant it to be read literally: as a expression of his desire and expectation, as a prod but not as an ultimatum. It was widely interpreted, however, as a not uncommon example of a *deniable* directive. Those responsible for Securities Centres feared the consequences of not meeting the deadline and acted accordingly.

Team leaders and doers agreed with the diagnosis that they focused on producing a quality product more than on speed but excused it by noting that this was what they had been led to believe was appropriate and that it was a function of the way in which TecSec worked. They further justified it by saying that lending managers were sometimes irresponsible in their willingness to expose the Bank to risk in the name of customer service. They quoted an often-heard statistic that perhaps 60 percent of the security taken by branches in the old days was flawed in some way and that 15 percent was unenforceable in law. These figures were officially denied, but there was suspicion in the Securities Centre that they were true and being covered up to prevent the Bank's embarrassment. At any rate, the problem was not that team leaders and doers were being overly fussy but, rather, that staff shortages, information technology deficiencies, new Bank policy, and lending managers' own inability to complete the requisition forms correctly were leading to delays.

Lending managers admitted that there were occasionally problems with the requisition forms that they sent in, but they felt that this was a minor part of the story. I heard three different diagnoses from lending managers and their assistants. The first was that the Securities Centre staff were incompetent and pedantic. The second (voiced by those who had visited the Centre or otherwise knew about it in detail) was that the Securities Centres were short-staffed, overwhelmed, and plagued by poor information technology. The third, not necessarily incompatible with the other two, was that the whole idea of Securities Centres was a bad one. As I discuss in more detail in the next section, this was seen by the Bank's executives as an illegitimate, defeatist diagnosis. As far as they were concerned, the idea that it was best to centralize securities work was not open for debate. What was in question was merely how best to implement that idea. Nevertheless, many lending managers maintained that they preferred having securities done in their branch or Corporate Business Group, which would allow them to have control over the process and also to ensure that their senior clerks would get some, but not too much, securities experience.

The regional *human resources* manager admitted that the appointment of the Centre manager had been a mistake but said that it wasn't his idea and that, anyway, they were easing the manager out as quickly as a replacement could be found. He argued that many of the fixed-term contract people were, in fact, better qualified than some permanent Bank staff hired during high-growth periods and said that the real problem was that, with the hiring freeze on, they were unable to convert enough of the fixed-term people into permanent staff. He diagnosed the human resources problems in the Centre as having two root causes—and this view was reflected in the review of the Centre produced by his department in September 1994: poor location of the premises and overly optimistic expectations of the information technology. The problem with the premises, he argued, was that there was not a surplus of staff of the required grades in the area where the Centre was located and that it was hard to convince people to move or commute in. Consequently, Regional Human Resources was facing a local staff shortage. The information technology problem was simply that the job had not been deskilled as much as had been promised; therefore, the very junior people whom he was tasked with finding were not, in fact, appropriate.

The Regional *Operations* manager admitted that the premises were less than ideal but said that he had been forced by a Bank policy of no new investment in property to use an available space and that this was the only one that was feasible. The original business plan was sound, he said, given what they knew at the time. His diagnosis mirrored almost exactly the list given above.

Information Technology admitted that TecSec was behind schedule and that there were problems with it and with the hardware on which it ran. The problem, it was explained to me, was money. Planned improvements to TecSec were prioritized below other information technology work, and twice in the past year their place on the priority list had been dropped still further as new projects had demanded attention and resources. The original plan had been to make TecSec a true "expert system," but that had been deemed by senior executives to be too expensive. The resulting heuristic system was as good as the Bank decided it could afford and would work fine when the planned improvements were made. The hardware was known to be inadequate, but the resources simply were not there to upgrade it at the moment. Hearing that I had spent time in the Centre, the manager I spoke to also said that, if I had met the Centre's manager, then I was no doubt aware that this particular Centre had problems other than information technology and that other Securities Centres were not having problems of the same magnitude as this particular one.

And so on. At one level, everyone agrees with the report. It is not necessary to scratch very hard at this superficial consensus, however, to reveal an underlying rash of conflicting claims about how the report should be interpreted and what conclusions ought to be drawn from it. One reason that everyone can complain in unison in BritArm and still nothing changes is that the unanimity underlying such complaints can be very thin, as we see in this case. Widespread agreement that change is necessary often masks deep disagreements about what should be changed and especially—given limited resources and limited managerial attention—what should be changed *first*. In a culture where a preference for avoiding conflict is not just widespread but institutionalized, this veneer of agreement does more than make the terms of debate harder to recognize. It provides a cover for avoiding having the debate at all. It allows people actively to misrecognize disagreeable disagreement. This cover is blown, however, if actions are actually taken to redress the problem. The underlying dissensus is then revealed: the actions—whatever they are—are unpopular with many and seen to be beside the point, or to reflect confused priorities, or, often enough, to make things worse.

REQUISITE CULTURAL COMPETENCE

The tissue of unanimity covering sharp disagreement is supported by two patterns of diagnosis in the Bank. The first pattern results from the importance placed on the diagnosticians admitting at least a small degree of responsibility themselves for whatever problem is being diagnosed. This gesture is required as a token of good faith and a signal that one is serious about fixing the problem rather than affixing blame. It is required to avoid defensive reactions. The issue is that, if one is seen to go too far in blaming other people, the diagnosis is discounted and treated as a deprecation, and then the strictures of tact and the stigma of being "not on board" apply. Thus, people in the Bank take great pains to be clear that they are "not looking to blame anyone, but . . ." Of course, culpability is framed in such a way as to facilitate it being explained away later, but, in the meantime, the illusion of consensus is sustained.

The second pattern lies in the illegitimacy of certain diagnoses. The fragile agreement about what *is* the explanation is bolstered by a strongly enforced agreement about what the explanation *may not be*. In this way, dissensus is bounded and radical views silenced. In the current example, the opinion that I heard from many lending managers that Securities Centres were not a good idea at all received a cool dismissal when I repeated it to the other parties involved. In part, this is because all the other parties are in some public way committed to the idea of Securities Centres—they thought of the idea, developed the implementation handbook, signed off on the business plan, developed the software, work there, or whatever. In part, however, it reflects the impact of hierarchy on diagnosis. Securities Centres are merely one part of what is known as *Delivery Strategy:* the Bank's plan to move all back office operations out of the branches and into increasingly fewer centralized paper factories. There is strong commitment to Delivery Strategy among the Bank's executives. The possibility of reversing Delivery Strategy and putting securities work back in the branches does not exist for practical purposes, I was told. For a middle manager to suggest it, then, is defeatist. It is merely an account, an excuse for not trying to solve the problems of the Securities Centres. Such defeatism was identified as part of the problem rather than part of the solution in a report by the cross-functional Securities Focus Group that described it as an "obstacle to change" deriving from "the existing branch culture of having a Securities Clerk in the branch." Thus do illegitimate diagnoses become framed as symptoms rather than solutions.

To see how the pattern of thin consensus was formed in the case of the Securities Centre, we need to set its diagnosis in context. Several formal reviews of the Centre in which I spent time and of Securities Centres in general were conducted in 1994. Besides the *Securities Focus Group Report,* the *Group Audit Report,* and the *Securities Centre Human Resources Review,* a consulting group was called in to produce a *TecSec Review,* the Centre's manager and senior assistant managers produced their own report and business plan, Regional Operations produced a *Securities Centre Organisational Report,* NS&D had a graduate trainee produce a report based on the *Securities Centre Implementation Handbook Questionnaire,* and the affected Regional Office produced a *Report on [This Region's] Securities Centre* and a *Report on Securities Centres.* Other regions no doubt produced their own reports about their own Securities Centres. There were also rumors of a high-level report being prepared for ManCo, the management committee consisting of the most senior executives of UK Branch Banking (UKBB).

Some of these reports were quite limited in scope; others, like that done by the Securities Focus Group and the Regional Office *Report on Securities Centres,* were more broad. The reports produced by outsiders—like the NS&D report, which concluded with the line, "I would stress to the regions that they should follow the handbook instructions," and the *TecSec Review,* which reported, "TecSec is perceived by its users to be a 'good', useful system"—were almost disarmingly obsequious toward the groups that commissioned them. Those produced by insiders were more predictable in their pattern of admitting fault, accounting for it, and finding fault with others. Taken together, the reports competed with each other for attention and created a noisy buzz of confusion around the subject that some concerned managers felt was being used as an excuse for inaction.

The diagnosis that I quote on pages 95–96 comes from a pair of Regional Office reports, *Report on [This Region's] Securities Centre* and *Report on Securities Centres,* that were produced as a response to that concern. They were dubbed *the Patton reports* after the credit risk manager who wrote them. Frustrated by the fact that previous reports had all been too narrow to give a complete diagnosis of the situation at the Centre (even that of the Securities Focus Group was too narrow since it concerned itself only with issues generic to *all* Securities Centres), the deputy regional director commissioned the *Report on [This Region's] Securities Centre* and selected Patton to undertake it not least because of his reputation for impolitic, blunt speaking.

In this, Patton did not disappoint. The clarity and bluntness of the report make it highly unusual among Bank documents. An example:

> The present manager does not appear to possess the necessary competencies to fulfill the role effectively. . . .
>
> The SAM [senior assistant manager] looking after the Manual Team gives the impression of having virtually declared UDI and is left to his own devices. There are hints of resentment in his not being involved in the main TecSec operation other than as a technical reference and he seems to have organised/managed his section in such a way as to prolong its existence.

The Manual Team refers to those clerks dealing with the partially completed security inherited from branches when they were taken on. Since these securities had been started on the old manual system, they were completed manually and then entered onto TecSec afterward. *UDI* stands for "unilateral declaration of independence." It is a common English allusion to Ian Smith's unilateral declaration of Rhodesia's independence from Britain in November 1965. In this context, it refers to the senior assistant manager running the Manual Team as a separate entity, without reference to the broader Securities Centre.

Patton is equally scathing (if syntactically somewhat cryptic) about factors external to the Centre that have led to its troubles:

> Referring to the Implementation Handbook it is clear that a lot of work has gone into planning for the centralisation of securities. It is a pity that this very detailed work was compromised by conflicting policies on premises and staff recruitment leading to the conclusion of "the best made plans of . . ." Unfortunately we have allowed known upfront costs for new premises and national policy on recruitment to overrule the Business Case. Leading one to question why we actually do such planning if implementation is to have its own agenda based on expediency.

In other words, having identified the specific deficiencies of the Centre's management, Patton then highlights systemic problems in the way in which the Bank routinely operates and calls into question its fetish for lavishly detailed plans that cannot be followed.

Not surprisingly, the report saw the light of very few days. Deemed likely to cause embarrassment and even offense, it was kept under wraps, copies were numbered, and it was not shown (formally at least) to any lending managers, to anyone in affected departments outside the region, or even to anyone in the Securities Centre. Indeed, I was put in the awkward position of having seen the report when none of my colleagues at the Centre had. They knew of it—it was begun with some fanfare, and Patton spoke to them in the course of preparing it—and were understandably curious about it, if (from my point of view at least) surprisingly unsurprised that they were prohibited from reading it. I heard later, however, that at least one of the senior assistant managers had been unofficially shown a copy.

Word leaked out of its existence, but more culturally appropriate documents were distributed in its stead. Patton was asked to write a second report, *Report on Securities Centres*, which left out all matters specific to this particular Centre and, thus, all specific references to individuals. It was this second report that was sent to the head of NS&D, the customer service director, and other interested parties. Each report was sent with a cover letter from either the deputy regional director or the regional executive director. An example from one such letter:

> All this originally stemmed from an awareness here that no single UKBB unit could be expected to accept "ownership" of the totality of the very many issues flowing from the establishment of Securities Centres, and the [This Region's] Centre in particular.
>
> Responsibility and accountability—to those who work in and use the Centre, and to UKBB—I felt had to be mine as RED [regional executive director]. It is "on my patch" [i.e., in his territory] and it gets us nowhere to seek to shift elsewhere most of the individual elements of responsibility.

A token of responsibility was, thus, added to the diagnosis before it was sent off.

Patton made it easy for those somewhat familiar with the situation at the Centre to read between the lines of his second report. It still contained a section on the Centre manager, for example, which now read: "Those SC [Securities Centres] who made an inappropriate appointment in terms of competencies will probably have fared worse than those who made better choices." Responses to the report ranged widely. At one end of the spectrum we have the polite and slightly patronizing letter from the deputy credit management director rejecting the suggestion made in the report that the culture of the Securities Centres be changed by having them report to Lending instead of to Operations:

Thank you for your letter dated 23 December enclosing a copy of Patton's findings.

I have also received a copy of Edward's [the regional executive director's] letter to Ted Grant [excerpted above] which quite rightly highlights the human element of the difficulties being experienced at Securities Centre. I know that it will not be seen as any comfort, but other Securities Centres are not experiencing so many problems. . . .

At the other end we have the more bluntly dismissive response of Doug Thomas in NS&D, who, when I met him for the first time, asked me if I have seen the Patton report. I said that I had and asked him what he thought of it. He paused and, looking cannily at me (a signal that he was about to be diplomatic), said that he found it "interesting." What he really wished he could see, he said, was the first draft, whose treatment of the management at the Centre was scathing. He laughed and said that he heard that it had to be cleaned up before it was sent out.

I asked him what he thought of the content of the report. It contributed to the debate, he said, but it didn't really have anything new in it, and what it mainly pointed to were the problems with Tom Phillips (the Centre manager): "He was the wrong man for the job, but now he is being used as a whipping boy and getting blamed for everything. I just heard that from Ward Candle [Tom's replacement], who says it is now the same with him: no regional support."

Doug's comment is interesting, not just because it suggests a devious mind (did Regional Office bury the first Patton report, not to save embarrassing the management team at the Centre, but to save embarrassing those who appointed that team and left them to fail?), but because it points back to the discounting of diagnoses that are seen as assigning blame—even if only implicitly—instead of finding fault. It is unseemly in the Bank to be seen as trying to pass off deprecation as diagnosis. Perhaps significantly, Doug Thomas had received his copy of the Patton report secondhand and sans context-setting cover letter. Having been presented with the diagnosis without an accompanying token of self-reproach on the part of the diagnostician, he reproaches the diagnostician. To mix metaphors, sometimes one must eat crow to save face in the unpopular culture.

The more diagnoses are phrased so that they are clearly not deprecations, however, the more they begin to seem like accounts: to avoid seeming to accuse, one often ends up seeming to excuse. What is more, one must always be aware of the politics of diagnosis and of which explanations will be dismissed out of hand as illegitimate. The result is that diagnosis is a mode of expression difficult to maintain in BritArm. To do so takes a good deal of cultural competence—a keen ability, as we shall see in the next chapter, to anticipate accurately how those in other subcultures of the Bank will interpret what you say—and the skills required are not the same, and may run contrary to, those needed to diagnose problems in the first place. The same bluntness and indiscretion that enabled Patton to clearly identify the problems with the Securities Centres enabled others in the Bank to discount his findings too easily.

This creates a dilemma for any would-be reformer in the Bank, a dilemma summed up nicely by one of the senior assistant managers in the Securities Centre: "You have to use the current culture to change it." In order to be heard and taken seriously, a deprecation or a diagnosis must be seen as legitimate; it must meet, in other words, the cultural standards described above. But the culturally provided ways of expressing negativity about the Bank are, not surprisingly, neutered. They reproduce the culture rather than provoking changes in it; they help people accommodate themselves to the status quo and position themselves within it.

This does not mean that the culture is self-sealing and in some permanent state of equilibrium. Rather, it means that, for explanations or criticisms to challenge the culture, they must be more than heterodox; they must be heretical. It is hard to be heard over the din of innocuous complaint when raising your voice is considered so rude that people may choose not listen to you if you speak loudly enough that they can hear. And, if they can hear and do listen, they may well disagree. As the conflicts among the various diagnoses of the problems of the Securities Centre illustrate, agreement with expressions of negativity about the Bank is strongest when those expressions are at their most vague and general. The more specific those expressions become, the more likely it is that disagreements will be exposed. In the next chapter, I look at the power that must be risked to be a heretic, at the capacity within the culture of BritArm to neutralize or marginalize even the loudest of blasphemous voices, and at the difficulty of negotiating between the different dialects of negativity in the Bank.

5

couNter culture

Estragon: I can't go on like this.
Vladimir: That's what you think.
—Samuel Beckett

When you walk into a traditional branch of BritArm Bank, the first thing you notice is the counter. In British banks, the cashiers sit on tall chairs behind the counter—and also behind the wall of thick bullet-proof glass atop it—to attend to customers. Traditionally large and imposing, made of mahogany, the counter divides the banking hall into two areas: one for the customer and one for the bankers. The customer side is small, sometimes consisting of little more than space enough for the queue where customers could stand and look through the glass, over the shoulder of the cashiers they were waiting to see, to watch the assistant managers, managers' assistants, and clerks at their desks doing the work of the Bank (managers having offices out of view). By the time of my fieldwork, BritArm was halfway through an ambitious remodeling program, dubbed FAME, or the Furniture and Merchandising Experiment, begun in 1990 to replace the so-called fortress-style mahogany counters with less imposing and more modern-looking (cheap-looking, complain traditionalists) counters made of synthetic materials. These new counters were set off to the side of the banking hall to leave more space for customers, and this new arrangement required that the back office functions be moved upstairs and, through Delivery Strategy, out of the branch altogether into Securities Centres, Service Centres, and Lending Centres.

There are fewer and fewer traditional branches left. In the course of shadowing managers, I toured several that were in the process of being remodeled or were just about to be. Invariably, the FAMEing of a branch triggered reminiscence and conversations that I enjoyed listening to about the old days when bank accounts were the privilege of only the relatively wealthy; when customers would tip their caps to the bank manager when they passed him on the sidewalk and would arrive deferentially, hat in hand, when requesting a loan; when ledgers were kept by hand and jobs were kept for life; when branches opened late and closed early and the manager lived upstairs; when formality was such that you would never call your manager by his first name, you would not take off your jacket without permission, and you would certainly not take the liberty of rolling up your sleeves. Much, it seemed to me, had changed in the past twenty-five years. What sense, then, could be made of the claim that nothing has changed in three hundred years?

I asked this question often, and the answers that I got varied. Some people pointed to things like remodeled branches and new technology as superficial changes, new backdrops for old behaviors. Others discounted the claim altogether, telling me that it is obviously false, just a cliché, "a thing to say." Most, however, argued that it is an exaggeration meant to make the point that things in BritArm are not changing as fast as people think they should. The Bank and its culture *have* changed, but, in the meantime, the expectations of customers and City analysts have changed more. There have been big changes to "the way things are done around here" in BritArm, but the changes to the ideal of how things should be done are greater still. This is a boon for complainers in the Bank: it means that, in some of the Bank's subcultures, there can be complaint about there being too much change to the culture going on and that, in others, there can be complaint about there being too little. That is, some complain that there is still too much of the old counter culture in the Bank and others that there is too much counterculture.

By 1990, top management felt that changing the Bank's culture was important enough to its financial success that "building a performance culture which constantly seeks the competitive edge in products, service, and distribution" was listed in the annual report as one of twelve elements of "the Way Ahead." In 1993, this was operationalized into a Vision (like *the Bank*, always capitalized when referred to) for the Bank: "To become First Choice for customers, investors, and staff." This effort, and the various culture-change programs launched in support of it, was largely met with cynicism from staff. But the cynicism took two very distinct forms. Some people were opposed to the idea of Head Office trying to dictate a new culture for the Bank. Others were in favor of the Vision but felt that top management was not sufficiently supportive of it.

We can see both these views reflected in the responses given to a questionnaire distributed in May 1994 in an effort to assess what progress had been made in achieving the Vision's aims. For example, a manager from the East Midlands writes: "I was very disappointed to discover 'The Vision' is mostly just the latest American Management Theory, re-hashed and repackaged, not our creation at all. If some MIT or Harvard Guru rediscovers the virtues of hierarchical management structures in 3–4 years, shall we have to put this all into reverse?" At the same time, an assistant manager in the West End of London writes: "[There is a] generally held belief that management at all levels, but particularly at more senior grades, neither practice nor have faith in the Bank's ability to achieve the Vision. Despite acknowledging the need for it in the face of increasing competition, the commitment shown towards achieving the Vision by management appears perfunctory. Until this situation is overcome, there seems little likelihood that the culture change required to bring about the Vision will succeed." Like the British press reports that agreed that BritArm's profits were bad but were divided about whether this was because they were too large or too small, so staff reactions to the Bank's efforts at culture change agreed that cynicism was in order but disagreed whether this was because it was a bad idea all too likely to succeed or a good idea all too likely to fail. What is more, many people fell into a third camp: taking comfort from their doubly negative view that it was a bad idea but likely to fail.

Just as the different reactions to Bank profits in the *Financial Times* and the *Daily Mirror* reflect the values and interests of these newspapers' audiences, so the reactions to the Bank's culture-change programs are not purely idiosyncratic. They reflect subcultural differences in the Bank. In order to understand the effects that countercultural complaint has (and does not have) in BritArm, we must first understand more about the pattern of subcultures in the organization.

Subcultures abound in BritArm: each with cultural elements unique to it; each with its own variations on shared cultural elements; and each with stances taken toward elements that it does not share. Nested, overlapping subcultures cover the entire organization and extend beyond the organization's boundaries. More like carpets strewn on a floor than like the tiles of a mosaic, these subcultures vary both in size (the subsection of individuals whom they cover) and in thickness (the subsection of the cultural inventory that they concern), and their edges are often fuzzy, not hard, fast, and straight. Far from being incidental to the overall culture of the Bank, subcultures are a defining characteristic of it. To treat them as "instances of specialized evolution departing from the mainstream base," as Hannerz (1992, 81) notes much of the anthropological and organizational literature does, is to get the temporal ordering backward in the case of BritArm.

The current organization was formed as the result of the merger of banks that together represent the amalgamation over 150 years of nearly two hundred private and joint-stock banks. BritArm traces its roots back to the seventeenth century since some of its acquisitions are that old. It was only in 1826, however, that legislation allowing joint-stock banks was passed. Prior to this, banks were privately held, typically with fewer than six partners (only with six or fewer partners could a bank issue bank-notes). This restriction had the effect of keeping banks small. It was shortly after the 1826 legislation that the major banks making up British Armstrong were formed. Over time, an organizational culture has formed, built in part around the mutual taking into account by subcultures of each other. The days when the defining characteristic of any manager was his employer before the merger are over, as are the days when decentralization was such that stark differences between offices and regions were allowed to persist. But subcultural variation and identity— defined, not only by corporate lineage, but also by geography, hierarchy, function, and age and in countless other ways—remain central to any understanding of how the Bank works.

In the last chapter, we saw that effective use of the various modes and forms of negative expression involves a degree of self-awareness—one's freedom to act is shaped by one's capacity for tact—but that, perhaps more important, it also involves developing a sensitivity to the perspectives of others. It requires an ability to make predictions about how others will interpret and react to a particular derogation, deprecation, account, or diagnosis made by someone like you in a situation like this (and, indeed, an ability to assess the predictions that others will be making about you and, thus, the intentions and expectations that they are likely ascribing to you). Will someone respond to you as a representative of the Bank? As someone working in Head Office? As someone who worked for many years in East Midlands? As a credit risk manager? As a former trainer at the Staff College? As a Yorkshireman? As a fellow cricket enthusiast? The cultural competence required involves a subtle understanding of the salience of speaker and subject to the various subcultures represented by his or her audience. This means guessing the perhaps one or two subcultures to which the audience member belongs that will be salient in the interaction, that the person will identify with in this situation, that will shape his or her perspective of it.

The guesses are not always correct. That is why introducing ambiguity and deniability, especially into deprecations and diagnoses, is so important. Cultural competence means being mostly right—guessing correctly the rough odds of how one's complaint or explanation will be taken— most of the time, not being perfectly accurate all the time. Ambiguity and deniability serve as a hedge against the embarrassment produced by acting on incorrect predictions. On the other hand, the fact that others are using ambiguity as well tends to make those predictions more difficult in the first place. Of course, all this is easier done than said, and, by describing it in terms of predictions and odds, we risk making it appear more deliberate and difficult than it is experienced to be by those in the Bank. As Bourdieu (1990, 93) says: "One can say that gymnastics is geometry so long as this is not taken to mean that the gymnast is a geometer." The lay ethnographers of the firm are not linear regressors, although the analysis of subcultures and perspective and identity can be described as a complex statistical calculation. The complexity is more analytic than phenomenological. For the culturally competent member of BritArm, there is nothing more straightforward, more transparent, than the calculus that we are discussing here.

In the past two decades, anthropology has made great strides in confronting the need to conceptualize what Hannerz (1992) calls *complex cultures*. These are cultures, like BritArm's or, indeed, Britain's, where differences of perspective between people are acknowledged to exist and culture is not perfectly shared. That is, people have some idea (correct or not) of these differences, and they try to take them into account in their contacts with others. This is in contrast to the ideally simple (and largely mythical) society where no differences of perspective exist and culture is perfectly shared. Whether or not Malinowski ([1922] 1961) and Evans-Pritchard (1940) were wise to treat the cultures that they studied as self-contained and homogeneous, there is widespread recognition in the field that ethnographers are not justified in these assumptions any more.

As Van Maanen and Barley (1984), note, these have never been safe assumptions in organizations. For one thing, no matter how alluring the metaphor may seem, organizations are very seldom like Goffman's (1961a) *total institutions*. People's perspectives reflect all the subcultures with which they are associated by virtue of the various roles that they play, both inside and outside the organization. Moreover, as perspectives are built up more or less cumulatively, they may reflect roles *previously* held as well. We may retain our attachment to a subcultural identity even after we leave the role that first afforded us that attachment. Rosaldo (1989, 194) puts it nicely: we are "more like a busy intersection through which multiple identities crisscross than a unified coherent self."

As a result, organizational cultures tend to be manifestly porous and variegated. It is perhaps ironic, therefore, that so much of our writing about culture in organizations borrows—when it thinks to borrow from anthropology at all—the classic "small-society" model that, in these days of global communication and commerce, is decreasingly seen in that field as applicable even to small societies (Baba 1989, 7). There are certainly exceptions, and Martin (1992, 155) is an example of a sophisticated approach to the issue of subcultures in organizations that acknowledges the fact that "subcultures overlap, they are nested within each other, and they intersect in the individual." What this implies is that the *sub-* in *subculture* not only refers to the fact that a subculture is made up of a subset of people from a culture but also concerns itself with only a subset of the whole cultural inventory. A subculture "need not encompass every aspect of the flow of meaning within this relational segment of the social structure[,] only what is more or less distinctive about it, as contrasted to the flow of meaning elsewhere in the same society" (Hannerz 1992, 71). Furthermore, subcultures may differ in the breadth of the cultural inventory that they cover. This means that subcultures can overlap and nest without contradiction because the clusters of meaning that they produce need not overlap or conflict. It also means that two people who are part of the same subculture (even, or perhaps especially, husband and wife) may nevertheless have different perspectives on different situations and activities because their various roles may mean that they are also parts of different subcultures.

Finally, it must be remembered that the defining characteristic of subcultures is their place in a wider whole. Thus, to understand the subculture, it is important to pay attention to what happens at the interfaces with the wider culture. Indeed, Hannerz (1992, 78) notes that "subcultures tend to be collectivized perspectives towards other perspectives"—the raison d'être of many subcultures is opposition to aspects of the wider culture. As Hughes puts it: "Whenever some group of people have a bit of common life with a modicum of isolation from other people, a common corner in society, common problems, and perhaps a couple of common enemies, there culture grows" (Hughes 1961, 28). Recall the Securities Centre and how the staff there came to identify with it as they were put in the unwelcome position of having to defend it. This is the norm: subcultures form in opposition to other subcultures. And, as Lamont (1992, 2) argues, the negativity and disapproval that members of one subculture express about another or about the generalized wider culture can be interpreted as boundary work, the patrolling of subcultural borders. This is how derogation helps strengthen group bonds: by more clearly delineating one subculture from the rest of the Bank. We saw that, for the purposes of complaint, the very definition of *the Bank* varies by subculture, typically indicating some diametrically opposed subculture. In branches, *the Bank* likely means the Head Office; in a given region, the other regions; among executives, regional, area, branch, lending, and administrative managers; among young turks, old dogs; and so on.

Because of the Bank's history as an amalgamation of different subcultures and the important role that subcultural variation and identity continue to play in it, it makes no sense to talk of a "mainstream" or "dominant" culture independent of subcultural influence. The dominant culture in BritArm has, in some sense, been constructed over time out of the mutual antagonism of its various subcultures.

Not all subcultures have or have had an equal hand in this construction. There is, to use a term that Hannerz (1992, 82) borrows from Mills, a *cultural apparatus* in the Bank. That is, there is a group of people and institutions whose role in the organization it is to produce culture, to provide meaning, to define the reality of situations—in short, to affect the ways in which others think. In general, the asymmetry of meaning provision mirrors the asymmetry of power in the organization. Those higher up in the Bank's hierarchy (i.e., those at the "Centre") have more influence over the dissemination of culture and have privileged access to media (think, e.g., of the official circulars and the Michael Cole videos that are sent to managers for the Wednesday morning Communication Meetings), thus creating the possibility of great asymmetry of scale and of long-distance cultural influence.

Much of the shared culture in BritArm derives directly from the influence of the cultural apparatus. But, in practice, this influence is not sure, and it is not straightforward. This is because the messages of the cultural apparatus are always interpreted from a perspective shaped by the various subcultures of which an individual is part: messages can become distorted or their impact diluted. It is also because the influence of the cultural apparatus does not depend on intent: those at the center of the Bank provide meaning for the organization even when they do not mean to. There is symbolic management in BritArm, but often the most potent symbols are those that seem unmanaged.

In this chapter, I examine the meeting place of BritArm's cultural apparatus and its subcultures, using several examples of the Bank's explicit attempts to change its culture. The discussion that follows focuses on three key issues: the ways in which all messages from the cultural apparatus are filtered and the difficulty of overcoming those filters while remaining true to a countercultural message; the difficulty presented to the would-be champion of a counterculture by the different dialects of negativity spoken by the various subcultures in the Bank and the tendency of each to reinterpret the messages of the cultural apparatus; and the subsequent need to use power to create change in the ways envisioned by these programs and the concomitant risks involved that lead the Bank's potential heretics to be reluctant ones. In other words, the chapter examines the ways in which the unpopularity of BritArm's culture both provokes efforts to change it and largely neuters those efforts, and it shows that, where that unpopularity does not prevent change altogether, it ensures at least that the changes are as unpopular as what they replace.

In a Raised Voice

The cultural apparatus in the Bank does not speak with a single voice. Observers of BritArm are not blessed with the luxury of Smith's (1990, 45–46) ability, for example, to talk unambiguously about "top management's attempt to restructure the behavior and culture of middle management" in her American Security Bank. And, conversely, BritArm managers are not cursed with an overbearing consistency of message so strong that "one branch manager could find no better term for the management philosophies, presented in the seminar and in the array of management literature distributed throughout the bank, than 'brainwashing'" (Smith 1990, 84). Far from it. The branch managers with whom I spoke in BritArm found many better terms—from *maddening* to *bewildering*, from *confusing* to *encouraging*. Each day, each manager will receive a pile of circulars with descriptions of new initiatives, updates on the progress of current initiatives, and, less frequently, obituaries of old initiatives. Confusion does not result just from the cacophony of contemporaneous culture initiatives introduced Bank-wide (ranging during the period of my fieldwork from Progressing the Vision to Organizational Culture Inventory to Performance Culture Inventory to Learning Culture Strategic Review to UK Branch Banking Core Values Programme) as well as more locally (a number of regions were doing their own culture and values work, as were Head Office departments such as Network Strategy and Development, with its Service Improvement Programme Values and Behaviours initiative). It results also from the plethora of other initiatives, programs, projects, pilots, and directives that overlap with or contradict the culture-change efforts.

The bewilderment can be overstated. Although initiative overload may be a favorite subject of derogation in the Bank, it causes few existential crises among managers. Simply having grown up in modern Britain is good preparation for it. More than a few managers said that they admired the tactics of a (likely apocryphal) colleague who simply put all circulars in his desk drawer without reading them, confident that, if any were important enough to warrant his attention, he would hear about them soon enough. But, for most, their Information Age skills of filtering, of selectively tuning in and out, of relying on a few proved (and usually informal) channels of information, and of reading between the lines made such drastic measures redundant. The problem facing the different elements of the Bank's cultural apparatus is, then, similar to that facing a British politician or adman: how to get one's message through, on its own terms, and have attention paid to it. This is a cultural problem, and solving it requires sensitivity to and adeptness with the current culture.

Consider, first, two of these initiatives, both associated with the Bank's Vision: the Organizational Culture Inventory and the Performance Culture Inventory. As the interchangeability of their names suggests, the two programs were strikingly similar. They were both run by Head Office departments—the "Corporate Quality and Change Management" Department in one case and the "High Performance Managerial Competencies (HPMC) Unit" of the "Personnel and Consultancy Services" Department in the other. I found it remarkable that the obscurity of these and other department names was not more often a target of derogation in the Bank. Both programs were running at the same time. Both had the aim of changing the culture of the Bank to create the attitudes and behaviors required to achieve the Vision of becoming First Choice. Both programs involved the use of outside consultants, and both assumed the possibility of quantifying culture and the necessity of measuring it against a predetermined ideal. The Vision being rather vague, however, it was not obvious what the ideal attitudes and behaviors required to achieve it were. The two programs settled on different ideals.

The *Organizational Culture Inventory* (OCI) was careful to claim that it determined the ideal cultural profile by "seeking input from a selection of Executives on the basis of known Vision aspirations." Coincidentally, however, the result of this input seeking was the determination that the ideal profile corresponded exactly to the generic profile of an ideal culture proposed by the consultants from whom the Bank had purchased the OCI. This ideal culture was one that was mostly "constructive" in its style of behavior, that is, one in which "members are encouraged to interact with others and approach tasks in ways that will help them meet their 'higher order' needs." This is in contrast to cultures that are "passive-defensive," ones in which "members believe they must interact with others in defensive ways that will not threaten their own security needs," or "aggressive-defensive," ones in which "members are expected to approach their work in forceful ways to protect their status and position."

After the ideal had been identified, a survey was distributed in October 1992 (i.e., before the Vision had been officially launched) to a sample of fifteen hundred individuals across the Bank, stratified by geographic region and grade of employee, asking to what degree different styles of attitude and behavior were required to fit in with the organization. According to a report prepared in 1994: "The results from this survey confirmed that the core culture at that time was particularly strong and oriented towards aggressive- *and* passive-defensive styles." In other words, the current culture was exactly antithetical to the ideal. In fact, it was so flawed that it reflected two antitheses of that ideal. The Bank's culture could be characterized, the report said, as resistant to change; valuing effort, not performance or achievement; a blame culture; nonparticipative, hierarchical, and bureaucratic; cynical and blocking; not open; and focusing on internal competition rather than collaboration.

Compare this to the *Performance Culture Inventory* (PCI). This program was based on the work of Schroder, Cockerill, and Hunt (1993) and defined BritArm's ideal culture as one that is customer focused and performance oriented, that encourages teamwork, and that achieves these qualities by virtue of managers displaying "high performance managerial competency behaviors." Nine of these behaviors were identified: quality improvement; proactive change; confidence in success; teamwork; strategic thinking; empathy; staff development; presentation; and influence. A questionnaire was devised to have subordinates rate their managers by indicating on a five-point scale their agreement with forty-five statements (five per competency behavior). For example:

> I feel doubtful about embracing the Bank's vision and values.

> We rarely discuss how the quality of our service can be improved.

> Information that conflicts with existing policy is ignored.

> We are encouraged to work together as a team.

> We are not stimulated by the presentations/communication meetings we attend.

The questionnaire was distributed to a sample of sixty-four hundred staff, again stratified by geographic region and grade of employee, in May 1994. A 62 percent response rate was achieved—sufficient, it was determined, to break results down by the Bank's nineteen regions and various Head Office departments, but no further.

In July 1994, each regional executive director received a copy of the Bank-wide results of the survey as well as an indication of how his region fared against the others (at the time, all regional executive directors were men). He was also given a short presentation on how to interpret the results and was instructed to ensure that all staff were informed of them. I sat in on one of these presentations where a staff member working on the PCI project, Jane Brooke, came to discuss the results with Edward Tollerton, one of the Bank's regional executive directors. Overall, the results were described as somewhat disappointing, with the mean rating across the Bank and across all the competency behaviors being 3.1 out of 5.0.

This showed, Brooke said, that the Bank starts from a reasonable point but has a lot of challenges ahead. The Bank scored best (3.75) on the dimension of quality improvement. This measured the degree to which "targets are set that focus on continuous quality improvement. This is the focus of the culture: a desire to do things better, a commitment to efficiency and quality." It scored least well (2.56) on influence: the degree to which "persuasive arguments are used to build support for ideas, organizational values and goals. Examples are set, and the desired behaviors are modeled. Influence is gained by the linking of positions to the needs of the group."

Tollerton's region had scored quite well in relative terms, ranking as the best region or within 0.01 point of the best region in six of the nine dimensions, and being above average in all nine. This was a source of satisfaction to Tollerton and to his managers, and, indeed, in the covering letter that he sent to branch managers along with copies of the results, Tollerton felt it necessary to warn against the danger of complacency and to encourage his managers to continue to work diligently to emulate the high-performance managerial competency behaviors. The use of so-called league tables in the Bank is widespread. These are lists showing how various parts of the Bank rank along specified dimensions. They promote competition among regions or within regions among business management areas or among individual branches. This is an ingrained cultural pattern and one that the people fashioning the PCI tapped in order to attract the attention of managers and to use their competitive spirit to improve the measures over time.

Significantly, not included in any of the published materials was a fact that Brooke revealed in her meeting with Tollerton: the sensitivity of the instrument was such that there was no statistically significant difference between scores that varied by 0.20 point or less. But, on average, the range between the best region and the worst was only 0.27. Brooke mentioned this fact by way of advising Tollerton that other regions were not far behind in their scores and encouraging him to work on improving his region's numbers to keep its relative position. By leaving out of the published reports this "potentially confusing statistical detail," as Brooke referred to it when I asked about it, regions that had performed less well could be more easily dissuaded from dismissing the rankings as so much statistical noise and admonished to work on improving their numbers to move up in the league tables. This would also make it easier to use the reports as a competitive measure contributing to the "balanced business scorecard" that measures the performance of each unit—as was planned for the future, when the questionnaire was to be sent out to 25 percent of employees every six months.

Promoters of the OCI were appalled at the use of relative rankings by PCI. Whereas the ideal cultures identified by the two programs were similar in most respects, OCI idealized a culture where different groups in the Bank collaborate rather than compete. PCI's tactics seemed to work directly against this goal. Furthermore, OCI saw as "aggressive-defensive" the "influence" behavior that PCI was promoting. OCI decried the hierarchical aspect of the Bank's culture and viewed culture as determined by what it takes to fit in with peers as well as leaders. PCI, on the other hand, reinforced the assumption that culture is itself hierarchical, with leaders' behavior determining the culture. The two programs thus became rivals, and a battle between them ensued. The war of words took place mainly in a series of memos and informal discussions with executives as both camps sought to secure support for their positions.

As part of the department responsible for the Vision and Change Programme, OCI felt that it had the legitimate right to determine the appropriate accompanying culture. What is more, OCI enthusiasts derided PCI for its assumption that merely raising consciousness and spurring competition were sufficient to induce change. As the senior executive in charge of OCI wrote: "This thinking is flawed: merely publishing the behavioral scores at the aggregate level will do little to encourage individuals to change. This comment is even more pertinent given the absence of developmental opportunities to assist Managers in understanding how they should change in order to move the PCI."

PCI supporters demurred, arguing that, although they expected PCI to bring about "improved workplace performance in the short term," they knew that the "development of a world-class managerial resource" was a long-term effort. Chief managers and executives had already been given formal training in the high-performance managerial competency behaviors, they said, and a booklet entitled *Measuring Quality Leadership: Examples of Contributions That Managers Are Making to Improve the Performance of Their Units* was made available to all managers. The booklet is a list of suggestions. For example: "Circulate questionnaires to each member of staff to ask 'what is the most valuable thing you do in your job?' and 'what is the thing you do which is of least value?' Eliminate all unnecessary activities." And: "Arrange staff visits, exchange between units (and customer businesses) to promote common identity or purpose and to build teamwork."

Critics of PCI argued that the "easier said than done" quality of this advice made it wholly inadequate for the task. OCI, on the other hand, was surrounded with a grand transformation program the goals of which included the creation and internal marketing of the Vision, Vision alignment conferences, learning centers, and mentoring, reflecting the belief that "it is the combined impact of a range of integrated initiatives that generate[s] the biggest and most sustained benefits." Indeed, the designers of the OCI program said that they had even bigger game in their sights: bringing other initiatives—such as the core process redesign, the service improvement program, the new grading structure, new performance measurement and appraisal processes, and the strategy and planning review—into the fold.

OCI won the battle. Its sponsors' desire that such things as performance measurement and strategic planning be made consistent with the new cultural direction of the Bank was rejected as expansionist, but OCI survived as an independent program. PCI, on the other hand, having been described in an April 1994 memo from the Bank's human resources director to managers as a tool that "puts us in a unique position compared to our competitors" and as being "the key to real, sustainable competitive advantage," was shut down six months later. To be more precise, PCI was not "shut down"; it was "re-positioned as a development tool." This meant that, if individual managers wanted to continue to use the PCI materials themselves, they were free to do so, but no further organization-wide surveys would be conducted. By the time of this repositioning, the previous human resources director had himself been repositioned.

OCI was left, however, with the problem of how to keep the attention of the Bank's management and staff and to demonstrate sufficient progress to keep the support of top management. To add weight to the contrast between the current culture and the ideal, OCI had in 1993 repeated its exercise of asking executives which behaviors (constructive, aggressive-defensive, or passive-defensive) they believed were most critical to the achievement of the Vision aims. It reported: "The results again cognated with the Verax model—and, in fact, were slightly more 'positive' than the Verax 'Ideal.' This indicates that the respondents had not only identified those behaviors needed to achieve a 'Vision' culture, but had identified the behaviors which were exemplary." Exemplary, maybe, but it is hard to make sense of a culture that is more ideal than ideal and harder still to take at face value the espoused belief that such a thing is critical to the Bank's "achievement." This result could, as OCI argued, reflect the stretching goals of executives who strive for more even than their culture consultants dare suggest. Or it could reflect the passive-defensive efforts of executives to thwart the project by failing to take it seriously.

A more general growing apathy toward OCI is, perhaps, evident in the fact that, after getting a 91 percent response rate to its 1992 survey of fifteen hundred employees, it was able to get only roughly 50 percent response rates to its follow-ups in 1993 and 1994 (including only one member of the Executive Team out of the eleven who had been sent the survey in 1994). Furthermore, by 1994, only small improvements had been made in the cultural figures that it was able to report. This did not surprise members of the OCI team, who told me: "We always understood that culture would take time to change. As a result, we did not attempt to include OCI within the operational scorecard as we knew it would be slow in moving, and in the absence of visible change year on year, would cause the business to doubt its progress and the organization's determination to move it longer term." Knowing that, in the Bank's culture, programs must show year-on-year results or risk being cynically dismissed or canceled outright, OCI tried to avoid reporting any results at all because of a belief that a successful culture-change program would not necessarily be able to show quantitative results in its first years.

Silence did not prove to be an option, however. In 1994, OCI was forced to communicate its results because of the increasing number of complaints received from questionnaire takers. The following is an example of one such complaint (as paraphrased by the member of staff who fielded the telephone call):

> She says she understands that the Bank cannot write to everyone when they have participated in research—but the fact which "really gets her goat" is that there is never any indication that staff views have really been listened to: "Why don't we get to see the results? What's the point of spending time and effort if we never get to know? I'm sick of wasting time on these things. I really don't believe that our views count. There's been no evidence of it whatsoever." [She] also mentioned that her branch is under a lot of pressure at the moment—short-staffed and so forth.

When the results were published, they were presented in comparative form (following PCI's lead and the cultural norm). Predictably, the first thing that the managers I was then observing did was to check how their region stacked up against those of their best and worst peers. This deflected criticism from OCI itself by focusing attention on relative scores rather than on overall progress, but, of course, it also had the effect of reproducing the aggressive-defensive style of competitiveness and opening the OCI program to charges of hypocrisy.

An interesting side note is that there was one group within the Bank that had shown great cultural improvement in 1993. This was the group of chief managers. The chief managers were middle managers responsible for a number of branches (approximately ten) in what was called a *business management area*. They were also responsible for a team of three to five corporate account executives who dealt with mid-corporate customers (medium-sized businesses with a turnover greater than £1 million per year), and many chief managers handled the relationships of the most important mid-corporate accounts in their territory themselves. They were singled out in the OCI report. Their exemplary attitudes were in large part the result of a program run by Tollerton, first for chief managers in his region and then expanded to include those in other regions, that encouraged participants to see themselves as the standard-bearers of culture in the organization.

The irony of this story is that, rather than the chief managers becoming role models for the process of culture change, their position was dissolved in the 1994–95 restructuring because it was felt to require too broad a set of skills to be manageable. This had an undeniable symbolic impact—emphasizing the increased specialization of jobs within the Bank and underscoring the restricted view of the abilities of BritArm employees taken for granted by the Bank's top management. It was a highly unpopular move—especially among chief managers—and cut against OCI's efforts to make the Bank more "self-actualizing." OCI could talk all it wanted about BritArm moving toward the desired outcome: "The organization values quality, excellence, innovation, and accomplishment—both in tasks and individual growth. Staff are encouraged to enjoy their work, develop themselves and take on new and interesting activities. Service and outputs are of high quality, and the organization attracts *and develops* outstanding employees." But the actions and business decisions of top management speak louder than those words. The 1994 OCI survey was conducted after the planned dissolution was announced, and the report indicated, with typical British understatement, that "particularly in the Chief Manager group . . . [there was] a complete reversal of perception compared with 12 months ago."

OCI faced cynicism and criticism from many corners. Its efforts reinforced two stereotypes of Head Office staff and their initiatives that were seized on by its detractors as evidence that its initiatives would fail just as previous ones had. The first stereotype is that people in Head Office believe that change can be effected through purely symbolic means. In fact, OCI did represent an attempt to effect change symbolically, but not by design. As should be clear from the discussion presented above, its sponsors hoped that decisions about restructuring, performance appraisal, strategy, and so on would be made with the creation of the new culture in mind. According to line managers with whom I spoke, however, the very fact that they pinned their hopes so high revealed their youthful inexperience and credulity. It reinforced a second stereotype: that of underage, overpaid Head Office staff sitting in London hiring even more overpaid and even less experienced consultants to help them think up bright new ideas that will inevitably prove impossible to implement. Head Office staff, it is said, believe that outside expertise is more useful than inside experience when searching for the solutions to the organization's problems. The opposite view is more common in the branch network, where experience is seen as essential and ideas are often denied legitimacy if they are seen to come from outside the Bank or to involve faddish management theories or buzzwords.

One real problem with BritArm initiatives is that, for the most part, the author of an idea is not the person from whom most staff hear about it. As a senior human resources manager lamented: "If only I could talk directly to each member of staff, I know I could convince them of our sincerity and that VIP [Valuing Individual Performance, an unpopular new performance-appraisal system] is a tool that can help them, not another bureaucratic formality. But by the time the message reaches the individual member of staff it has gone through so many layers of management, many of them steeped in the old culture, that it has lost its meaning." In an organization the size of BritArm, merely to reach all staff of management grade required an exhausting ordeal by Michael Cole of repeating over and over his impassioned speech about the Vision to crowds at the Staff College. The rest of the staff received their understanding of the Vision from secondary sources, such as videos shown in Wednesday morning meetings, and took their interpretative cue from their manager or someone else. A full year after the announcement of the Vision, an announcement accompanied by great fanfare, 100 percent of staff polled were aware of the existence of a Vision, but only 59 percent knew without prompting that it "had something to do with 'First Choice.'" The media, as always, was a source of power for the cultural apparatus, but an uncertain one.

To ensure that OCI and the Vision and Change Programme of which it was a part were not ignored or dismissed as just another initiative, threats were made. For example: "There will be a place in the Bank only for those who are 'on board' with The Vision." Indeed, psychometric tests were administered to senior executives to assess the degree to which they were "on board" and test scores distributed so that each manager could see how he rated against his peers. There was great debate among top management about how and whether to use these test scores. They were never explicitly used for their threatened purpose of determining promotion and demotion among executives. Nevertheless, the scores focused attention and cut through the clutter with dramatic effectiveness. They did, however, have the obviously undesired side effect of reinforcing the utility of the aggressive-defensive behavior that OCI fretted was in danger of being considered "the desired norm" for the Bank and of undermining the nascent constructive style of humanism (where the "organization is managed in a participative and employee-centred way") that was supposedly "critical to the achievement of our Vision aims." This is the dilemma of using the current culture to change it: the techniques most culturally effective in getting people's attention have the side effect of reinforcing elements of the culture that are targeted for change.

A caution is in order. In this examination of the influence of the (unpopular) cultural apparatus, I have, to some degree, been speaking as if the audience were undifferentiated. That is patently false. I met Vision *true believers* (a subcultural label assigned by the *Vision cynics*), people who had been moved by Michael Cole's speeches at the Staff College and who pined for the day when the deadwood of senior middle management would be swept aside and a new guard would join him in revolution. And, even where there seemed to be a unanimity of cynicism and derogation about the culture or the Bank's efforts to change it, this sometimes hid a diversity of views. Earlier, I quoted Goffman (1974, 575) as saying: "When we are issued a uniform, we are also issued a skin." The skin of cynicism and derogation is accepted as all the more authentic in the Bank because the uniform of ideology seems artificial (being "on board" or else), but it is just as much a cultural provision. And, in a reversal of Hannerz's (1992, 107) caveat that there may be public compliance with the ideology of the cultural apparatus without private acceptance, there can in BritArm sometimes be public cynicism and derogation despite private acceptance and belief.

Role distancing here, then, involves the display of *positive* attitudes toward the Bank, and it is common because of the stigma attached to being considered a complainer. Not surprisingly, the opposite is common too. We have seen the functionality in the Bank of derogation in breaking conversational ice, in eliciting sympathy and understanding, and in bringing a group together in solidarity against a common enemy. These are examples of a bonding function valuable enough that, as did the inmates of St. Elizabeth's that Goffman (1961a, 63) studied, BritArm employees will occasionally hypocritically join in derogation merely to keep up appearances among an in-group, just as they will occasionally hypocritically join in condemning derogations to keep up appearances among an out-group that they do not wish to displease (a peer group that they do not want to insult, e.g., or a hierarchically more senior group that they may wish to join).

Dialects of Negativity

The next culture-change effort on our docket was undertaken by Edward Tollerton in his region of BritArm. Tollerton was a popular man in the

Bank, extremely so with those who worked for him. The performance of the region from 1988, when he took it over, to 1994, when I conducted my observations there, was widely recognized in the Bank as exceptional in terms of key performance measures such as the growth of the region's operating contribution, sales of related products per customer, cost-income ratio, and cost of risk. Tollerton had a keen interest in issues of organizational culture, learning, vision, and values as expressed in the writings of Edgar Schein and Peter Senge. Bill O'Brien, the former CEO of Hanover Insurance, who features prominently in Senge's (1990) *The Fifth Discipline,* was a friend and mentor of Tollerton's and came to the region to speak to managers there. It was this interest in management theory, and Tollerton's success in applying it in the Bank, that explains why he was chosen by BritArm's CEO to participate in the Bank's work with MIT and how I came to know him and to center my fieldwork in his region.

Tollerton's strong belief in the link between good business performance and vision, values, culture, and learning, however, generated a mixed reaction among his peers and superiors (there are two levels of management between Tollerton and the Bank's CEO). Although many of his fellow regional executive directors respected him deeply, one or two were cynical about his ideas and resistant to any suggestion that he should be held up to them as a role model, either directly or through their chief managers via the expanding training program that Tollerton ran. Likewise, some of the Bank's executives, including its CEO, felt that he was, indeed, a role model—as indicated, for example, by his being asked to design and run the Chief Managers' Workshop and by my being sent to study his Region—whereas others hinted to me that they did not agree with what he represented.

Tollerton, who had worked in the Bank his whole life and whose father had worked for the Bank before him, had strong opinions and a deep affection for the organization. Because he was approaching the mandatory retirement age and, therefore, had no expectations of further advancement in the Bank, he also felt it easier to speak his mind about Bank policies than did the younger colleagues who expressed private agreement with his sentiments. To my ears always almost circumlocutory in the politeness with which he expressed his ideas, he nevertheless found himself from time to time falling short of the Bank's high standards of tactful discretion, and this occasionally caused friction. As we shall see, shortly after the primary period of my fieldwork, Tollerton retired, and the organization was restructured in a way that effectively shut down the changes that he had worked to achieve and moved his region unambiguously back in line with the rest.

Tollerton's attempt to create what he called a *Value- and Vision-Led Approach* is revealing of the difficulties involved in leading an attempt to change a subculture from the middle of the organization and the contradictions that arise from the fact that the responses—or potential responses—of several key subcultures must constantly be taken into account. The Value- and Vision-Led Approach contrasted with the *Command and Control* management style prevalent in much of the Bank. When Tollerton took over the region, he started by discussing with his section heads (i.e., regional sales, human resources, operations, and lending directors) and chief managers what sort of region they wanted theirs to be, what their values were or should be. As he describes it, once those shared values had been articulated, the region's employees could work together steadily to embed and to live them. From this discussion came a one-page document, a statement of the region's aims and principles. This was later elaborated on in a booklet written by Tollerton entitled *Our Operating Values*.

Seven values were identified: *our colleagues; our teams; our customers; BritArm as a banking group and as our employer; localness; leanness;* and *openness*. For the most part, the values are consistent with the "constructive styles" described by OCI. However, three of the values are unique, and these three are interesting because they reflect a self-consciousness of the region as a subculture and of the power of the cultural apparatus. They are BritArm as a banking group and as our employer, leanness, and localness. We will look at each of these three in more detail.

The statement "We value BritArm as a banking group and as our employer" is elaborated on as follows in *Our Operating Values:*

> We focus on being a business with obligations to shareholders as well as to customers and colleagues. Complacency will become a dangerous enemy for us unless we work to a philosophy of continuous improvement.
>
> We need always to remind ourselves we are a business. We care about ourselves as a Group and want to have pride in BritArm. We must always want to be better. There is something bigger and more important "out there" than ourselves or our own Branch or Unit. We must do things to develop and nurture a "Group Attitude."

The question to ask of this value is: Why it is necessary to say that the region values BritArm as an employer? Can this not simply be taken for granted?

There are, I think, two reasons for this. The first is the perceived strength of subcultures in the Bank and the competition between them. It is thought to take an effort to nurture a BritArm "Group Attitude" because attitudes and allegiances are more often local (to the branch, the region, or, perhaps, the entire branch network as opposed to Head Office). There is an often-repeated sentiment that people find the morale in their unit high but believe it to be low across the Bank. A respondent to one of the Bank-wide culture questionnaires put it succinctly: "Staff love the Branch, hate the Bank." That this quote comes from an assistant manager in another region is evidence that this is not a phenomenon unique to Tollerton's group. Although loyalty to BritArm as a whole is easily shown to outsiders, inside the Bank loyalties tend to be expressed more locally. To an internal Bank audience, it takes an effort to "have pride in BritArm." This is not something that comes naturally (or culturally).

The second reason is the region's awareness that it is a subculture, not a culture unto itself. By this I mean that one of its defining characteristics is that it is but one region of fifteen. Central to its subculture, then, is a perspective on other subcultures and the cultural apparatus. Equally central is a sensitivity to the perspectives taken of it by other groups in the Bank. As Tollerton described things, it was important to make clear that the region was "on board" with BritArm's style and policies and, later, its Vision as well and that it was not trying to be different than other regions. To take any other stance would be culturally unacceptable and would undermine the region's efforts.

This value, then, is a signal to other subcultures in the Bank that the intent was not for the region to go its own way. If the message is not received, Tollerton makes it more explicit in *Our Operating Values* and elsewhere: "We never set out to be different to any other region, and part of me always feels uneasy when I hear the Region spoken of in that way." Indeed, in letters to audiences outside the region, Tollerton—sometimes with tongue firmly planted in cheek—goes to great lengths to show how the Value- and Vision-Led Approach is, in fact, nothing new for the Bank and merely an articulation of what BritArm has long practiced. For example: "BritArm, through its historic paternalistic culture, has always tended to see itself as a value-led organization, even though those values may not have been written down. This in many ways is still our strength and we have seen that strength used in, for example, the way in which difficult redundancy decisions have been implemented, with concern expressed for the individual and for the reputation of the Bank. Nothing in this paper should be taken as suggesting this is not recognized." Although not disingenuous, this is only a partial truth. Tollerton expressed to me many times the belief that, at its best, BritArm operated according to a set of implicit values, values that he admired. Just as often, however, he expressed the opinion that the Bank all too seldom was found at its best and that all too often it operated according to a style of command and control that he did not want to replicate in his region. He reconciled these views by explaining that, were the Bank to articulate its values as the region had done and undertake the same process to try to embed them, it would more often operate according to them.

By 1993, however, the Bank's Vision and its values had been made explicit through the Vision and Change Programme and OCI, and Tollerton had an even finer line to walk. He had to show those outside the region that the region was fully supportive of the Vision while also seeking to explain to those inside the region why *Our Operating Values* was not redundant. He did this by emphasizing the consistencies between the Vision and the region's values and arguing that, because of the Value- and Vision-Led Approach, there would be no need in his region for the strong-arm tactics considered for use elsewhere in the Bank to ensure that people were in alignment with the Vision. Indeed, he argued that it was more important than ever to reemphasize that the region's values were genuinely consensual, not imposed. This was because he felt that the power of shared values to shape behavior in positive ways was destroyed if the values were forced on people.

Tollerton could not say this explicitly, however, without being seen to compare his region favorably with other regions, so he had to be more oblique. Casting his justification as a critique of the way in which the Vision and OCI were being implemented was far less risky than critiquing either the content of the Vision or the way in which it was being received in other regions. So he claimed that his region's values had continued relevance in that they helped overcome new uncertainties. For example:

> It has been said that people do not so much object to "change" as such, but rather to "being changed by others." In so far as much of the change is being, indeed has to be, prescribed with required ways of doing things under the BritArm Vision, a sense of being constantly pushed forward and into enforced behaviour changes is now present amongst many staff. Communications making it clear that there will be a place in the Bank only for those who are "on board" add for some people an element of threat. There is uncertainty about the Bank's prime objective; about our values.

Subculture-change programs in the Bank are, as we see here, complicated by a lack of audience segregation. Documents such as *Our Operating Values* are distributed, not just intraregionally, but also interregionally, and they make their way to the Head Office as well.

A similar dynamic of speaking to two groups at once underlies the next value that I want to consider: leanness. It is described as follows:

We run a "tight ship." We don't spend money on appearances and show unless there are good and well thought out business reasons to do so. We make our assets and our advantages work for us.

Leanness rather than meanness means continually increasing our capacity to produce more higher quality results with less resources; and having a pride in doing so because it is right. There is more to this than simply aiming to cut costs. People react adversely to meanness which has a selfish connotation. Systems Thinking and a true understanding of leanness will incorporate a willingness to spend to achieve something beneficial, even though it may mean waiting for those benefits.

This definition is purposefully vague because Tollerton wants to appeal to two separate, and conflicting, perspectives among those in the region about what sort of changes are needed in BritArm. These two perspectives belong to subcultures that one Bank wag called *the Thatcherites* and *the Labourites* of BritArm.

The Thatcherites see tremendous fat and waste in the Bank's operations and feel that strong measures are called for to cut costs and firm performance metrics required to shape up or ship out laggards. They fear that managerial softness, backsliding, and inertia threaten the chances of real change in the Bank. Patton, the author of the *Report on Securities Centres* (one of the so-called Patton reports described in the last chapter), is the stereotypical Thatcherite. His recommended method of changing the culture of the Securities Centres stemmed from a belief that "money often speaks louder than any words in achieving objectives, not only in relation to culture, but also in terms of efficiency. If the manager and assistant managers in the Securities Centre were to be paid by results, then we would quickly see dramatic improvement in performance."

It is to this group that Tollerton writes in *Our Operating Values:* "The sort of value-led approach set out in this paper is on occasions described—quite wrongly—as 'soft,' implying that it can provide excuses to avoid tough and unpleasant decisions which may be necessary to achieve business performance in difficult conditions." In doing things like justifying the region's planned expenditure on "corporate health and culture" to Head Office, he had to make similar justifications. In facetious response to a skeptical query about these particular investments, Tollerton wrote: "That the reaction was to describe [the aim of these proposed expenditures] as 'motherhood' we took as a compliment, the quality of motherhood probably having the greatest influence on a human's subsequent contribution in adult life."

The Labourites, on the other hand, see neglect of opportunities for investment in revenue growth in the Bank's focus on cost cutting. They are concerned about the human impact of policies such as the hiring freeze and argue that cuts often affect customer service by short-staffing the branches, hurting morale, and creating a vicious cycle of cynicism and anxiety. They voice the often-heard complaint that the Bank's Vision unduly favors investors and, sometimes, customers and that scant attention is paid to the espoused goal of being First Choice for staff. They feel themselves to be part of a silent majority, but not in power, and not possessing a powerful voice. It is to them that Tollerton speaks when he twice emphasizes that "leanness is not meanness" as he tries to strike a balance between two perspectives both of which have elements with which he agrees.

The danger is that the balance is reached at the expense of this particular value actually standing for very little and the definition of *leanness* being essentially vacuous. Tollerton said that he hoped that vagueness in the abstract was compensated for by clarity in the pattern of concrete decisions that he and his managers make. In that case, however, the purpose of articulating the values in the first place is called into question. The point is that Tollerton (or any agent of change in his position in BritArm) must negotiate, not only between differences of perspective between those inside and those outside his region, but also between subcultures represented within the region itself.

The third value of interest is localness:

> There are different ideas as to what constitutes localness. It is not about local units gaining control, or having more authority based on power, nor does it mean decentralisation per se. It is about being clear who is best placed to make decisions and have views listened to by those who may be required to make central decisions.
>
> Centrally, we are often reluctant to seek local views because they may not accord with what we want to do. We give doubtful reasons, such as "confidentiality," or a genuine belief that "Head Office (or Region) knows best!" We are often unable to trust decision-making to local people because we may lack confidence in them, forgetting that experience, and the confidence of others, in themselves, produce learning and improved skills.

Here, again, is a balancing act between promoting a degree of empowerment and advocating heretical levels of decentralization. What is interesting is that this statement reflects the assumptions about culture change embedded in the Value- and Vision-Led Approach. If OCI assumes that a large-scale, centralized culture-change program is necessary, and if PCI assumes that revealing the culture to people and measuring their progress at changing it is enough, Tollerton's approach is antithetical to both OCI's and PCI's. Unlike OCI's, it is local and unprogrammatic; unlike PCI's, it neither reveals the current culture nor measures progress toward a new one. As we saw, however, those programs were as they were for pragmatic reasons. If you believe in empowerment, what do you do about the situation where people empower themselves to ignore your calls to empower those beneath them? If you believe in democracy, what do you do if people freely vote to abolish it?

In other words, Tollerton's approach is local not just in the sense of being initiated regionally instead of Bank-wide. It is also local in its approach to culture change in the sense of promoting empowerment where possible over top-down control. Tollerton insists to his section heads and chief managers that there is no real contradiction: "It follows that, in our own leadership roles, not only must we seek consistently to practice those Values in which we believe, we must also do all we can to see they are practiced by others, most of all by our immediate subordinates. This is not being prescriptive; we are talking about consistent, value-led, leadership. Not to discharge our responsibilities as leaders in this way can itself come to be seen by others as not practicing what we would claim to believe in." There is a difference, Tollerton argues, between empowerment and abdication of responsibility. Yet he notes that, if he is to practice the localness in which he claims to believe, he must be "willing to leave Section Heads and Chief Managers and their units to restructure the operating values if, in that way, it is likely to lead to a better result. The spirit of Our Operating Values is very much more important than the words themselves." Left open is the question of who decides whether "it is likely," but the idea is that section heads and chief managers are encouraged to live by a set of consistent, articulated values and that they must ensure that their subordinates do so as well. Just which values, exactly, is (formally) left for each manager to decide.

Our Operating Values was never circulated to all staff, although it was available to anyone desiring it, and its brownnosing utility was well understood by all staff in the region. Of similar utility was Senge's *The Fifth Discipline*. Finding the book accessible, valuable, and consistent with what the region was trying to achieve—and certain that many of his managers would as well—Tollerton was torn between a desire to proselytize and his sense that "if we are to use the book as an effective learning tool we shall best do so by creating circumstances in which individuals are curious and keen to obtain it. We must avoid simply introducing it by giving it to people. In doing so we could run the risk of it being seen as prescribed reading, leading to prescribed behavior." Because his appreciation of the book quickly became well-known—it was widely rumored (only half jokingly) that he always kept copies of the book in the boot of his car just in case he met individuals curious or keen to obtain it—those who asked for a copy or, much worse, explicitly referred to it in meetings or discussions were often teased later as having done so to suck up to him, and a few of his managers took evident pride in their display of independence of thought by refusing to express the slightest interest in obtaining a copy. Through derogation, in other words, some cynical staff exercised the degree of localness that they possessed even before it was elevated to the status of an operating value.

For Tollerton, managing this seeming paradox between prescription and empowerment was simply a part of what good management was about. It meant acting at times, as he was not afraid to do, as a shield protecting his managers from the commands and controls of Head Office that were inappropriate to local conditions or that would have unintended consequences running counter to the goals of the Bank—empowering them, in other words, to do what was right for the business. At the same time, good management also meant vigorously enforcing those commands and controls that were inviolable and necessary. Most of all, however, it meant having the wisdom to know the difference between the two. In the organizational world, where people are routinely fired for breaking the rules but where unions can threaten to "work to rule" in the knowledge that such behavior will bring operations grinding to a halt, Emerson's words were never more true: "A foolish consistency is the hobgoblin of little minds, adored by little statesmen and philosophers and divines." Ambiguity and inconsistency are the manager's hammer and sickle.

There is an important ambiguity inherent in *Our Operating Values.* The booklet is written in the present tense, as if the region already possessed the seven values that it outlines, yet these values are described as "aims" and as being in need of future adoption in the region. The explanatory text is carefully left equally ambiguous: "As with all lasting cultural change it takes time, and is more likely to be achieved if the new order can be built out of the existing deeply embedded corporate and personal values which govern people's motivations and behavior." This ambiguity was nicely captured in the name of the document preceding *Our Operating Values:* that is, *The Region's Aims and Principles.* When I asked Tollerton about this title, he said that he had chosen it without much deliberation, that it just sounded right. In the document, the aims were never explicitly separated from the principles; each item mentioned both. Similarly, the operating values are described as "representing Values appropriate both to the Bank's historic culture and the sort of organization we might aim to be." They are the once and future values of the Bank. As Tollerton puts it, they are created "out of, but not inhibited by, the cultural strengths of the past, and therefore more likely to be long lasting."

This usage points to a common, although not universally held, view of

the Bank's culture. It is not exactly nostalgia but a belief in a positive cultural core or history that has become twisted and distorted but that can
be reclaimed. Such an explanation of affairs can serve long-serving and
loyal BritArm managers as an account of why they stay with, and even
love, a Bank that they nevertheless feel is worthy of the derogations and
deprecations made of it. It is also a framing of culture change that ap-
peals to those who prize experience over outside expertise. It balances to
some degree, then, the strong influence of American management theory that Tollerton's managers perceive in the Value- and Vision-Led Approach. The price paid for this balance is that the future/present ambiguity can also be derogated as an excuse for inaction. Tollerton notes:
"At times in the past we did feel ourselves obliquely criticized with the suggestion that we may have felt we had done all there was to do. If that were
ever so, it would represent the very antithesis of what we are about. We
should be both arrogant and complacent and would be on the downward
slope."

The challenge of protecting against arrogance is real, as is the challenge of protecting against accusations of claiming to be different from
other regions. The "It is different here" account, discussed in the previous chapter, was very common in this region. People in the region talked
often about it being different from (better than) other regions, and the
performance figures supported this assertion. Recall, too, the finale of the
Regional Office Christmas pantomime, where it is not until the region's
statement of aims and principles is added to the UK Branch Banking Vision that Michaelstein is able to come to life. Such symbolic displays are
at once a source of satisfaction to Tollerton and a source of anxiety.

Overall, reconciling the perspectives of the many different audiences
with which he was faced was clearly an impossible task for Tollerton. The
ambiguity in the description of the targeted operating values provided
some margin of error for the balances that had to be struck. It allowed
thin agreement on some values to be enough to achieve compromise. To
protect against those on which there was not even rough agreement, ambiguity of intent was added to ambiguity of target. The approach's deprecating intent was made deniable by the description of *Our Operating Values* as both aims and principles, the approach itself as both diagnosis of
how the Bank already operated and statement that, indeed, it should operate that way. Such finely tuned ambiguity proved fragile, however, because, as with all meanings provided by the Bank's cultural apparatus,
in some ways it complemented and in some ways competed with other,
also officially sanctioned voices, initiatives, and change programs. Despite
Tollerton's repeated insistence that his approach directly contradicted
nothing being said by those higher up in the Bank's executive, it was seen

by advocates as doing more than merely complementing the Bank's official line. To the extent that it competed successfully for attention and adherents, it belied its own message of innocence.

Ultimately, the tightrope that Tollerton was forced to walk proved too slippery even for someone of his practiced diplomatic skills. A restructuring of UK Branch Banking was announced that included the elimination of the chief manager and regional executive director positions. Tollerton regretted this change. He viewed the regional executive directors and the chief managers who reported to them as natural focal points for the Value- and Vision-Led Approach. As I described above, he had achieved success in his workshops with chief managers—from both his region and others—getting them to see themselves as the standard-bearers of culture in the organization. The regional executive directors, Tollerton included, were not consulted before this change was announced. This was not surprising: neither rule nor precedent obligated the Bank's executives to follow a participative approach, although, in practice, such consultation had been far from unheard of in the past.

Tollerton spoke up against the restructuring in a senior management meeting. Prefacing his comments by assuring those present that, whatever his private views, he would work diligently to ensure the success of the restructuring if it went ahead, he then argued that the purported benefits of the change (greater accountability of managers and cost savings) could be better achieved, and with less disruption, in other ways. His remarks met with a cool reception, and he was encouraged to keep them to himself. Tollerton's position—that he had principled objections to the proposed changes that reflected his experience and local knowledge but that he would ultimately work hard to implement whatever new structure was decided on and imposed—ran against the more typical pattern in BritArm of securing local loyalties by derogating exactly those decisions by "the Bank" like the one to restructure and was considered untenable by many in the Bank. They preferred that Tollerton quietly fall into line.

The restructuring went ahead as originally planned, and, conveniently, Tollerton was due to retire only a few months after his job would be split into two roles: one focusing on retail customers and the branches, the other focusing on midcorporate customers. With his agreement, his retirement was brought forward by three months to accommodate the transition. I came back to England for Tollerton's last week—to catch up with my various informants, to interview Tollerton's successors, and to attend his retirement party. The party was a special and enjoyable occasion, marked by fond remembrances and the sad emotions of separation. I found the mood in the day-to-day operations of the Regional Office, however, to be dark, and the region's managers expressed fear and uncertainty about the future. Rumors and conspiracy theories floated around and attached themselves to most anything.

The region had been known for both the size and the quality of its lending book, for example, so, when internal auditors arrived about that time, rumors abounded that they had been called in because certain people in Head Office considered the region to be "out of control" and wanted it brought back in line. These conspirators hoped, it was said, to find evidence of irresponsible lending by the region's managers. Perhaps, it was hinted, they would manufacture that evidence by being overly stringent in their application of the rules if they could not find it fairly. As a result of the investigation, the region was forced to make extra provisions for bad and doubtful debts. Within two years, over 75 percent of these provisions were written back—meaning that they had been unnecessary—vindicating the region's lending practices as having been sound. At the time, however, the provisions were highly symbolic and were used to justify the views of those who thought that the Value- and Vision-Led Approach should be retired with Tollerton.

Six years later, the facts of this episode remain elusive: Was the audit routine or extraordinary? Was it fairly conducted but misleadingly over-cautious, or was it unfair and calculated to send a certain signal? Aside from my coming back to ask questions, there is little speculation about it anymore. The region was vindicated in the end, and Tollerton is widely remembered with respect and affection. But, although there is still evidence here and there of elements of the Value- and Vision-Led Approach, it has disappeared as a force for change. The conspiracy theorists at the time might or might not have been right about the mechanism, but they were right about the outcome. The region was brought back into line and now looks and sounds like the rest of the Bank.

The feeling of intense drama at the time made it a difficult moment for me personally as well. In my meetings with Tollerton's former subordinates, I was asked by several to do what I could to help ensure that the region would be allowed to retain the Value- and Vision-Led Approach. The situation was complicated by the fact that, under the restructuring, Tollerton's role as regional executive director was eliminated and his responsibilities divided among two people. Neither of these two successors was seen as value or vision led by people in the region. Rather, both were seen as ambitious (not a compliment in BritArm, as we have seen). Things reached their dramatic zenith when one manager pulled me aside to tell me (with no touch of irony): "I and many others in the secret army are counting on you in this, John. We owe it to Edward if not to ourselves." These requests shook me. They overestimated my influence with the Bank's CEO and top management generally and misunderstood my role as an ethnographer. They estimated and understood all too well, however, my personal debt to Tollerton for the access and resources that he had given me and my deep sympathy about the situation. Although I was certain that there was nothing that I could do, it was hard not to feel that my inaction was a form of betrayal.

Derogation on High

The question is raised: How serious is the Bank's top management about changing the culture of the organization? Certainly, I heard no more sincere complaints about the Bank's culture and explanations of why it needs to be changed than I did in my interviews with the CEO and his subordinates. Receiving each day a packet containing photocopies of all the articles in the press relating to the Bank, top management is regularly reminded of the views of analysts in the City and the newspapers that the Bank's bureaucratic culture weighs it down and prevents it from moving quickly enough to cut costs and generate new ideas for revenue growth. Keep in mind, however, that the complaints at the center of derogations are just as sincere, and must be just as valid, as those expressed as deprecations. The question is not whether the complaint is genuine; it is whether it expresses a desire for redress. Here, things are less clear.

Given the overwhelming sentiment against the Bank's culture, as it is seen, and the nature of its unpopularity, to defend it is to take a stance that is itself difficult to defend. An individual who stands up for the culture or ignores it as an important issue is less likely to be seen as a courageous and independent thinker than he or she is to be framed as so much a product of the Bank's "culture of complacency" as to be blind to its flaws. One can stand up for particular beliefs or practices, but the culture as a whole must be deprecated. Just as there are risks at lower levels in BritArm of being seen as too stiff or too strange to complain about the Bank, so those risks remain at the top. The difference is that the received wisdom about organizational culture is that, to the extent that anyone can change it, it is top management that can. Therefore, whereas culture is the ideal bogey of complaints and explanations of negative outcomes lower down in the Bank because responsibility for any number of modern ills can be shifted to it, the calculation is different in the rarified air of the executive suite. If one complains about the culture there, as one must, one must also be seen to follow up those words with action of some sort.

However, organizational culture is also commonly considered—inside and outside the Bank—as being heroically difficult to change. It would be rash indeed, and unnecessary, to stake one's professional reputation on an ability to change the culture of BritArm. Furthermore, organizational culture is thought to be easier to make worse than to make better. In a banking environment, where customers are assumed still to prefer a staid brand that projects security, trustworthiness, conservatism, discretion, and wealth, the necessary ingredients for fostering the entrepreneurial spirit are potentially dangerous. When I asked, for example, why branch managers could not be given more discretion about the layout and operation of their branches, I was greeted with kind-spirited laughter and gentle reminders of my naïveté. The customer demands a uniformity of look and procedure, I was told. "We can't have branch managers putting up whatever signs they want in the windows," one senior manager told me with a shudder not unusual among his colleagues. "Before you know it, they'll be having 'going out of business' sales."

Assumptions about the British banking customer also underlie certain trade-offs that the Bank feels it needs to make: "If someone comes into the branch to find out their bank balance, they don't mind waiting a bit for the answer nearly as much as they mind getting an answer that is even just a little bit wrong." Precision is more important than efficiency. In chapter 4, I recounted the responses that I received to my questions about why deprecation could not be more forthright: laughter, again, and references to what it means to be British. I also asked many people why the Bank's operations required so much hierarchical oversight. Why could individual managers or units not be trusted to manage their affairs responsibly and then be assessed on their performance at the end of the quarter or year? People were, after all, supposed to be the Bank's most important asset. And this oversight seemed to me an important cause of the bureaucratic red tape, inflexibility, and centralization in the Bank. More laughter was the most common response, followed by allusions to famous stories of hidden trading losses and embezzlement or analysis of how few bad loans it would take to wipe out the Bank's profits completely. "Money is not like other commodities," one manager told me in a typical response. "It creates more temptation and presents more opportunity for, mmm, *irresponsibility* than other commodities."

Laughter is revealing. It occurs when a comment violates an assumption that is taken for granted as obviously true. Underlying the macrolevel cultural patterns of bureaucracy, centralization, lack of innovation, and so on, then, are deeply held assumptions—what Schein (1992, 26) calls *basic beliefs*—in the Bank about the nature of banking, of money, of human nature, of Britishness, and of BritArm itself. Changing those remains unthinkable, too absurd and dangerous to consider.

What we might expect to find, therefore, is the offloading of the management of culture from executives themselves to various programs and teams who are given the responsibility of changing the organizational culture but the authority to act only at the symbolic level. They are given the unenviable task, in other words, of changing macro-level cultural patterns through purely symbolic means. In order that everyone may appear serious about the concerted effort to change the culture, these programs will be given sufficient financial and symbolic support—speeches, exhortations to the troops. What they will be denied is structural support. The basic assumptions of the current culture will continue to direct the day-to-day decisionmaking in the Bank. There is some evidence for this in BritArm.

The chief manager role, for example, was abolished without concern for the impact that this might have on efforts to make the culture more self-actualizing. More generally, no concern seemed ever to be paid to the signals sent by the cultural apparatus through its actions. OCI was rebuffed in its efforts to correct this. The imperative to cut costs and improve accountability led to a laundry list of initiatives and a major restructuring from a geographic to a product orientation that were enacted in such a way as to reproduce aggressive- and passive-defensive styles and reinforce the notion that constructive styles of behavior were a luxury affordable only when the business was on a sound footing, not a prerequisite for that soundness.

Take, for example, the Core Process Redesign (CPR) project. Teams were formed in Head Office to map the routine processes of Bank operations, optimize them, and then "roll them out" as prescribed behavior across the Bank. Cost savings were anticipated from such innovations as forcing managers to handwrite their interview notes with customers (so that fewer typists would be needed) and partially automating the job of reviewing the "out-of-order" list of overdrawn accounts by using information technology to strictly enforce rules about when checks should be bounced. Current practice had managers' assistants using their judgment about when to call customers to ask them to put money in the account right away to cover the check rather than simply bouncing it and imposing a fine. Under the new system, all such exceptions were automatically logged and required written justification. By its centralized nature, however, CPR worked against the constructive ideal and reinforced the passive-defensive habit of dependence. Further, many of its innovations were regarded by staff as directly contradicting the Vision's aims of First Choice for staff and for customers. The argument that reducing costs would not just boost the share price but also allow BritArm to improve its service by reducing charges was made by the cultural apparatus, but it fell far short of convincing the Bank's many cynics.

For BritArm to have a culture-change program is undeniably useful to executives and the Bank as a whole in its dealings with the outside world.

It demonstrates a realization that cultural complacency is unwarranted and a commitment to change. More important, it frees up culture to be used by top management as a target of complaint. It legitimates negative lay ethnography for the uses that have been discussed in previous chapters: the euphemization of power; strengthening bonds; assigning blame. The point, however, is that, just as the usefulness of derogation does not depend at all on the complaint being redressed, the usefulness of culture-change programs seen in this light does not depend at all on their changing the culture. This cannot be admitted without destroying the effectiveness of the tactic, but it can be observed.

It can equally be observed that, despite all this, the culture of BritArm has changed in significant ways in recent years. Modes of thought about careers have been altered by the end of the promise of a job for life and the specialization of career paths as back office work has been moved out of the branches and into centralized "factories"; assumptions about the nature of branch work have changed in response to new sales quotas; expressions of teamwork have changed as the retail and midcorporate sectors have been segregated and a transfer pricing scheme established to mediate between them. To these changes can be added the myriad small ways in which an organizational culture such as BritArm's changes all the time: in response to new leaders, to new influences from the wider culture outside the organization, and to the dynamics of its own internal evolution. No culture is static. It is not the *reasons* for the unpopularity that persist— these were always differentially distributed among various subcultures anyway—just the unpopularity and its manifest patterns of derogating, deprecating, accounting, and diagnosis.

Indeed, the fact that the culture of the Bank is changing and (how else?) for the worse has itself become a useful derogation, as a final example illustrates. To make tactfully clear to the manager of the Securities Centre that his performance was not acceptable, a regional section head took the approach of explaining to him "that the culture of the Bank as we knew it has changed, and is going to continue to change, and a major change of approach and development of new skills would be required for [him] to go forward in the position of Manager of the Centre," so perhaps he ought to reconsider early retirement. The manager, incidentally, declined the offer and stayed in his job for months before finally being "repositioned" in less tactful terms. Never mind *plus ça change, plus c'est la même chose*. In BritArm, the more things change, the more unpopular they become.

6

Lɑy ethNogrɑpHy

All people have a right to the culture they prefer,
regardless of whether it is high or popular.
—Herbert Gans

A commitment to the principle of cultural democracy is not a conspicuous feature of the literature on organizational culture. The idea that employees have a right to the culture that they prefer cuts against the widespread assumption that management has the right, indeed, the *duty*—if not necessarily the *ability*—to shape the culture as it sees fit. Employees are not born into the organization, and they are free to leave it if they do not like the culture. The management self-help literature explicitly endorses this "my way or the highway" stance, with Peters and Waterman's (1982, 77) comment that employees can "either buy into their norms or get out" reflecting a general view that cultural democracy in organizations is essentially a matter of voting with one's feet. What is more, central to this literature is the assumption that organizations do not typically have the culture that their managers should want for them. Organizational cultures, these books argue, all too often reflect the uninformed preferences of existing and past employees rather than the interests of the organization and the likes and dislikes of the sort of people whom its managers should want to recruit and retain. Culture is, if anything, *too* democratic. It is a manager's job to change that.

The academic literature has often been critical of this normative orientation, exposing managerial manipulation of culture as a form of "corporate tyranny of the mind and heart" (Kunda 1992, 225) that is not more insidious and dangerous only because it is seldom as effective as managers would like. Arguing normatively in favor of cultural democracy, this literature reflects descriptively the same ambivalence about the actual possibilities for cultural democracy that we find in discussions of popular culture—and for the same reasons. When Van Maanen and Kunda (1989, 91) argue that "managers may define what is given, but the managed will define what is taken," they echo Gans:

> I cannot subscribe to the notion that popular culture is simply imposed on the audience from above. I believe that it is shaped by that audience, at least in part, albeit indirectly. The mass media, and perhaps all of commercial popular culture, are often engaged in a guessing game, trying to figure out what people want, or rather, what they will accept, although the game is made easier by the fact that the audience must choose from a limited set of alternatives and that its interest is often low enough to make it willing to settle for the lesser of two or three evils. (Gans [1974] 1999, xiii)

This similarity is no coincidence. Business organizations share with books, television, and the cinema the property of being exit-option democracies. Everyone has a choice—at least theoretically—but only a few have a say. Mass media and management are both examples of a cultural apparatus with undeniable, but uncertain, symbolic power. They create the same dynamics, and they raise the same issues.

In each case, what we are interested in is the relation between the provision of cultural artifacts—be they the staging of Broadway plays and the poetry of rap music or the staging of company retreats and the poetry of corporate mission statements—and the underlying values, beliefs, and preferences of their intended audiences. Do the persisting artifacts of culture reflect the preferences of many or the power of a few? We know that, in the abstract, the answer always lies somewhere in the messy middle between those two extremes. People are not cultural dupes, but their preferences are culturally shaped; real choices exist, but those choices are always constrained, and much of culture passes beneath the level of conscious choice.

Knowing this does not stop us from asking where in the middle particular cultures lie. Indeed, that question has never been more interesting, in part because, in these resolutely relativistic days in cultural sociology and anthropology, identifying a culture as having been imposed, and, thus, as inauthentic, is one of the few reasons considered legitimate for judging one culture more negatively than another. The ethic of cultural democracy runs deeper than relativism in the common wisdom: all people should have the right to the culture that they prefer without the undue influence of socially powerful elites, economically powerful cultural imperialists, or politically powerful leaders. If they do not have this, then we can depreciate the culture as inauthentic. If they do have this, then, as Berger (1995, 30) says, we seem to have no legitimate grounds for disagreement if they assert: "My (sub)culture is just as good as yours."

What if instead, however, they assert: "Our problem is our culture"? How do we respond then? So long as everyone is assumed to be basically ethnocentric, democratic relativism is not only a helpful epistemological stance but also a good tactic for conflict avoidance. When people complain about their culture, however, and compare it negatively to others, it is a hard stance to sustain. If we agree with them that their culture is worse than others, we contradict the fundamental principle of cultural relativism that cultures are incommensurable. If we disagree with them and insist that their culture is no better or worse than others, we succeed only in contradicting a different principle of cultural relativism by privileging our understanding over theirs. By opening our mind, relativism seems to tie our tongue. And what of cultural democracy? Are we to take the complaint about the culture as an indication that the managers and employees of BritArm do not, in fact, have the culture that they would prefer? Or is that complaining best understood as an expression of their preference for just this sort of culture, one where complaint is ubiquitous? Does the idea of cultural democracy make any sense at all in a culture of complaint? In the next two sections, I examine these issues in turn.

Relativism and Unpopularity

The question of how to respond to the negativity about the culture in the Bank is not merely hypothetical—I was confronted regularly with this dilemma during my time in the Bank. Because I was known to be studying culture, I was often asked what I thought about the Bank's culture and whether I agreed with the complaints. There are only two ways to respond: recant relativism, and either agree or disagree that something is wrong with the culture; or remain silent. Confounding expectations by remaining silent is hard to do, but, done once, it is at least easy to do well thereafter. Trying to answer the question on its own terms produces quite the opposite experience: it seems easy enough at first—and early in my fieldwork I found myself offering all sorts of opinions, often mutually contradictory, when asked about the culture—but soon proves untenable.

REASONS TO AGREE WITH THE COMPLAINT

If you are known to have even a modicum of experience with BritArm Bank, it is hard to claim with any credibility that you have no opinion about its culture. Everyone seems to have an opinion—employees, customers, even the people who check passports at Heathrow Airport—and all these opinions seem to be negative. Perhaps there is no puzzle here, no need for complicated analyses of why people in BritArm complain or for fine distinctions between derogations, deprecations, accounts, and diagnoses. After all, we do not think twice, and certainly are not compelled to complex analysis, when somebody complains after having had her wallet stolen. Perhaps the reasons that people in BritArm complain about their culture are equally the self-evident result of their objective conditions.

Certainly, people in BritArm have compelling cause to complain. Their industry, once a cozy oligopoly, has become increasingly competitive with the entrance into the retail banking market of everyone from former building societies (roughly equivalent to thrifts in the United States) with better public images, to beloved retailers like Marks and Spencer who are now selling financial products, to American competitors launching direct-mail campaigns and offering credit cards with aggressively competitive rates, to branchless Internet and telephone banks with lower costs and sexier products. Customers—especially the most profitable ones—once deferential and grateful, but now increasingly demanding and fickle, may flock to these new competitors with better brands and better products. The Bank's bureaucratic culture is too inflexible to allow the rapid cost cutting needed to compete on price, not entrepreneurial enough to compete on product innovation, and too inward looking and not customer focused enough to compete on quality of service. That is why the culture is a problem. Or so Bank staff were told in Vision briefings and Wednesday morning Communication Meetings. Discount the current profit figures, take them with a grain of salt, because the truth is that BritArm is ill prepared for the threats that loom on the horizon.

During the six years that I observed the Bank, its revenues and profits went up and down, but these looming threats for the most part stayed on the horizon. Building societies like Abbey National have drawn away some market share, but they have also found that, by becoming banks, they have managed to attract the same sort of public and media criticism that hounds the traditional High Street banks like BritArm. Marks and Spencer, the retailer famous for its high-quality own-brand prepared foods and also for its underwear, remains a small player in the financial services market. On the whole, BritArm's customers, if not loyal, have at least proved to be fairly durably inertial. New entrants to the market like Egg, the e-commerce subsidiary of Prudential, have found that competing aggressively on price to win new customers has won them mainly price-sensitive customers who have not proved profitable. That certainly does not mean that these competitors, or others, will not eventually seriously undermine BritArm's performance. It does mean, however, that justifications on performance grounds given for complaints about the culture are not self-evident—even if they are widely accepted within the Bank as valid.

Threats to the Bank, however, need not affect financial performance to have a material impact. The fact that industry analysts in the City believed BritArm to be vulnerable because of its high costs and its staid and complacent culture was reflected in the Bank's share price. Its financial performance meant that the Bank was never in any danger of going bust, but, if it failed to address the concerns of analysts and its share price weakened, it could be in danger of being taken over. As we saw in chapter 2, this was a hard message to sell to employees. The possibility of being taken over seemed remote, and the consequences if a takeover did occur were uncertain. In contrast, the cultural consequences of the Bank's attempts to cut costs and improve performance seemed clear and immediate and worthy of complaint. Old assumptions about job security and career advancement no longer held. The centralization of processing out of branches and into paper factories was making jobs more specialized and deskilling many of them. The typical branch manager now had fewer staff, less autonomy, and fewer responsibilities than his or her predecessor and was afforded no more prestige by customers than the manager of the local supermarket. These outcomes were unpopular. Indeed, it is difficult to say which was more common: negativity about the culture justified by the Bank's performance—including the performance of its share price—or negativity about the culture justified by conditions created as part of the effort to improve that performance.

This highlights the fact that, even if it were self-evident that one organizational culture led to better performance than another, it would still not be clear that one was preferable to another. We need not rely on Bourdieu (1984) or Lamont (1992) to tell us that people may value elements of culture more than they do money—let alone the money of shareholders. In the end, five years after I had finished my full-time participant-observation in the Bank, the fears of BritArm's executives about a takeover were realized. After a major strategic blunder sent its share price falling, the Bank was acquired, and, to a man (there were no women in BritArm's top ranks), the entire Executive Team was removed by the new owners. The very scenario invoked in so many Communication Meetings to inspire the sense of urgency and concern thought to be needed to change the culture came to pass. By all accounts, however, the Bank's middle managers and staff did not actually seem to mind. In my interview with the chairman of the acquiring bank, I was told stories of BritArm managers warmly welcoming their new leaders, who were delighted to find, instead of hostility or defensiveness, a penchant for telling tales of how bad things were in BritArm and an attitude that the acquisition could hardly make them worse. In meetings with BritArm pensioners, the new owners were loudly applauded. My discussions with old informants suggest, however, that within a year of the merger—once BritArm employees began to feel a part of the new organization—complaints about the new bank were as ubiquitous as of old.

"I think the clever part of the BritArm deal," one City analyst was quoted as saying in *BusinessWeek* magazine, "is that [the acquiring Bank] realized BritArm was struggling but not a basket case—they had a lot of strengths" ("Is This Europe's Best Bank?" 2002). That it took cleverness to see anything positive about one of the country's largest and most consistently profitable companies with one of its best-known brands says something eloquent about the negativity infusing the Bank. What will happen to the culture in the Bank, and to the pattern of complaint about that culture, is a question for future study. Ethnography is not a predictive science. The only conclusion safely drawn here is that we are further than ever from being able to establish self-evident grounds for agreeing or disagreeing with the complaint about the culture. Both the criteria chosen on which to compare cultures and the judgments required to apply those criteria are themselves culturally specified. Or, more accurately, they are subculturally specified: as we saw in chapter 4, different parts of the Bank have different, often mutually contradictory, ways of justifying their negative views about the culture, as do outside constituencies.

REASONS TO DISMISS THE COMPLAINT

Even though we cannot determine objectively whether the complaints are, in fact, accurate, we might still have reason to dismiss them as mere noise. After all, in chapter 4 we saw evidence of how much loyalty and even love many employees hold for BritArm despite their complaining. We saw that the derogations of the Bank do not signal an earnest desire for change or even disaffection. We saw that some of the complaining is for show, that people admit in private liking the Bank more than they feel comfortable admitting in public. We saw that, even when people are earnest about their expressed dislike for elements of the culture, this is sometimes balanced by an acceptance that these are things that they must nevertheless live with because it is unrealistic to expect change and equally unrealistic to expect that they could find work in an organization that was significantly better. Moreover, in chapter 5 we saw that there is a great deal of commitment within the Bank to certain assumptions about the nature of banking, of money, of human nature, of Britishness, and of BritArm itself that underlie the macro-level cultural patterns of bureaucracy, centralization, and lack of innovation that attract negativity. Indeed, so much of the complaint about the culture seems to have been directed at such functions as bonding and blaming rather than at communicating truths felt about the culture that perhaps it makes little sense for us to take the content of the complaints seriously.

In its pattern of self-depreciation and the tactful avoidance of embarrassment, the culture of BritArm reflects the broader British culture in which it is set. Perhaps this suggests the most parsimonious explanation of the complaints about the Bank: To complain is simply to be British. That is, complaints are not meant to be taken too seriously but are merely a manner of speaking. Perhaps we risk making too much of it and making a mistake similar to concluding from a preponderance of "How do you do?" inquiries that we have discovered a culture of people with an unusually heightened concern for the health of new acquaintances. Harold Macmillan, the former prime minister, once said of the English: "We know that on the whole, in spite of all our self-depreciation, this is the finest country in the world" (quoted in Paxman 1998, 131). Can the same be said within BritArm? Do the complaints disguise the high regard that employees, in fact, have for the Bank? The answer is not straightforward. It is certainly the case that the culture of BritArm reflects many elements of broader British culture. But it does so in exaggerated form, like a funhouse mirror. In short, BritArm is more British than Britain. It reflects a stereotype of that national culture, one consistent with the Bank's position squarely within the British establishment. BritArm is not unique in its unpopular culture, but neither is it uniquely British. All organizational subcultures borrow from the national—and regional and occupational—cultures in which they are set. They do so selectively, however, and not without recontextualization. Both BritArm and, say, Virgin are recognizably British companies, but they highlight quite different facets of the rich, complex, and multilayered national culture that they share.

Further, although it is true that much of the complaint in the Bank demonstrably does not signal an earnest desire for redress, some of it does, and, as we saw in chapter 4, all complaints must be justified, must be considered valid, if they are to help perform the bonding, blaming, and other functions of negativity that we have identified. It is not the case that one can freely complain about anything at any time and escape sanction. New employees learn quickly that clear and direct deprecation may be hazardous to one's health. More subtly, in a culture where a common complaint is that there is altogether too much complaining going on, considerable cultural competence is required to know how much complaining is too much. One must master the difference between a derogation that brings people together in affirmation of shared suffering and one that is mocked as a whinge; between a deprecation that subtly makes its point and one whose true meaning is either so hidden that it is missed or so naked that it is reproved; between a diagnosis that attributes enough blame to the speaker to shift the rest to someone else and one that is either too self-damning or too self-righteous. The form and the content of the complaint matter considerably and must reflect shared sentiment if the complaint is to be accepted as valid.

In other words, we cannot understand the complaints if we take them literally, but neither can we understand them if we reduce them to their "objective" reality as efforts to break conversational ice, strengthen group bonds, shift blame, express status, or euphemize power. The duality between being meant as valid complaints and yet not always being meant as complaining is essential to the phenomenon. The literal meaning of the negativity must be justified for any secondary meaning to be accepted. Complain about something in a manner or at a time considered unjustified—complain overmuch about your company car or be insufficiently positive about a proposed restructuring, to take examples discussed in chapters 4 and 5, respectively—and your literal meaning will not be overlooked and will not be gotten over; you will be teased or reprimanded. Derogations, deprecations, accounts, and diagnoses must be recognized as literally valid for their "real" effect to be misrecognized and their function performed in the deniable fashion required. Therefore, we can no more understand the negativity in the Bank by dismissing it as disingenuous than we can by taking it at face value and searching for the objective, or at least self-evident, grounds on which to evaluate it.

REASONS TO REMAIN SILENT

The important point about the complaints made within the Bank about the Bank, and the reason that silence is the best answer to questions of whether we agree with them, is this: The people making them are not talking to us. This is the nature of lay ethnography. The term *lay ethnography* is a presumptuous one inasmuch as it seems to mark a distinction between those who have been trained in ethnography and admitted into its holy orders and those who have not. Cast this way, it raises the hackles of those of us whose ethnographic training has predisposed us to believe that, in the face of the impossibly high standards of faithfulness, clarity, and grace to which we would like to aspire, we are none of us professionals but all amateurs of varying and uncertain quality. This is, anyway, not the distinction that I have in mind. Rather, with the term *lay ethnography* I want to distinguish between ethnography that belongs to the people and that which does not, that is, between descriptions of a culture created by and for the people of that culture and descriptions aimed at an audience that includes people outside the culture being described.

The difference is significant. About nonlay ethnographies—perhaps we should call them *ordained ethnographies* to make the distinction clear—Van Maanen writes: "They sit between two worlds or systems of meanings—the world of the ethnographer (and readers) and the world of cultural members (also, increasingly, readers although not the targeted ones). Ethnographies are documents that pose questions at the margins between two cultures. They necessarily decode one culture while recoding it for another" (Van Maanen 1988, 4). Ordained ethnography, then, is the attempt to make one culture intelligible to another. Lay ethnography, on the other hand, is an attempt by one culture to make sense of itself. For those of us outside the culture, overhearing the lay ethnography, it is data, not description. This is not because of a presumed hierarchy of understanding that privileges the insights of the academic ethnographer over those of the natives. The difference between ordained and lay ethnography lies, not in the question of the authority of the speaker, but in the question of the identity of the intended audience. As interest in culture and cultural differences has increased, natives of many kinds are taking up pens and soapboxes to explain their cultures (or subcultures) to others. Some of these ethnographic efforts will doubtless be judged better than others, but all will be ordained in the sense of being attempts to render one culture understandable to another.

By saying that lay ethnography is, to the outsider, data rather than description, I mean simply to highlight the fact that people talk differently about a culture when speaking among insiders than when speaking to outsiders. Lay ethnography is spoken in confidence. Not necessarily in confidence that it will not be repeated, but in confidence that it will be understood as intended. Among insiders much can be assumed. Assuming shared experience, winks and nods, nuance and connotation—the complicating elements that thicken the description in ordained ethnography—can be taken as understood in lay ethnography and need not be explained. Likewise abbreviations, jargon, and shorthand references to shared memories. The language of lay ethnography is *emic;* it is part of the world that it seeks to explain. Moreover, assuming shared identity, boasts and complaints, half-truths and exaggerations, can be spoken in the confidence that they will be set in context and not taken too literally. Of course, especially in a complex culture such as BritArm's, bountiful in its subcultural diversity, these assumptions never hold entirely. The distinction between who is an insider and who is an outsider is seldom a binary one—a fact that makes participant-observation feasible. There is always a degree of ambiguity that creates the possibility for miscommunication but that may also be exploited, as we saw in chapter 4, to create new forms of expression with certain advantages of tact and embarrassment avoidance.

Field-workers are, in a sense, professional eavesdroppers. Ethnography, however, is not gossip. Its task is not merely to report artifacts noted, behaviors seen, and conversations overheard. Ordained ethnography must also provide the context necessary for its audience to understand what those artifacts, behaviors, and conversations mean to those inside the culture. The ethnographer does not transcribe the culture; he or she *inscribes* it: noting what was not said as well as what was said; uncovering assumptions and pointing out connections evident to cultural insiders; making explicit the tacit knowledge of the culturally competent. Ordained ethnography, then, deconstructs lay ethnography—and the other elements of culture observed during fieldwork—to render it intelligible to an outside audience.

This is necessary because, even when the lay ethnography is in the same language as the ordained ethnography, it is part of a different language game. People in BritArm learn to complain differently about the culture depending on the different subcultural identifications of their audience within the Bank, and they speak of the Bank very differently to those outside it. Far from being a matter of duplicity, this is a requirement of integrity. The same complaints about the same things have very different significances and are interpreted in very different ways in different contexts and when made to different people. Take the guffaws about the Vision videos and the other gentle jokes at BritArm's expense discussed in chapters 2 and 4. When spoken within BritArm, these display affinity with the Bank and strengthen local loyalties through their affirmation of shared suffering. To an outside audience, on the other hand, the identical words may signal distance and disaffection between employee and organization and invite unwelcome criticism of the Bank from a public already perceived to be hostile. We have seen that this same pattern holds among the subcultures within the Bank: to make the same impression and have the same effect across audiences (to strengthen social bonds, e.g., or request redress, or deflect blame), different messages must be delivered. This is why the question to ask of ordained ethnography is not whether it contradicts or is consistent with the lay ethnography of that culture— it is aimed, after all, at different audiences and with different ends in mind—but whether it *explains* it and how well.

Democracy and Unpopularity

Whatever its demerits as the basis for moral theory or investment advice, then, cultural relativism is the only tenable stance from which to study lay ethnography. To understand the unpopular culture in BritArm, we are best served, not by *evaluating* the negativity about the culture in the Bank, but by examining the *role* that this negativity plays in the culture and the *rules* that govern its use. In particular, it is interesting to consider the extent to which the rules constrain the roles and call into question the idea of cultural democracy.

LAY ETHNOGRAPHY AS POLITICAL ACTION

Complaint serves several purposes in BritArm. We have seen how, with requisite cultural competence, complaints about the Bank can be used to warm up conversations among relative strangers, to strengthen group bonds, to account for untoward actions or events, to shift blame. Ostensibly, complaints are expressions of discontent or dissatisfaction, and it is true that, in order to perform any of its various functions, the complaints must be considered valid. Validity, however, does not depend on the complainer actually feeling the discontent or dissatisfaction that he or she is expressing. Rather, it hinges on the opinions of the audience about the complaint and the person making it. The complaint is valid to the extent that it reflects the shared understanding of the situation and is made by a member of the group in good standing. Thus, much of the complaint in BritArm about the Bank expresses identification more than it does alienation.

We cannot reliably treat the complaints about the culture as if they were a form of voting against the culture. Complaints are not votes, and, even if they were, they might better be seen weighing *in favor* of the culture. If cultural democracy operates at all, it does not operate this way. People do not select culture at the macro level, choosing among candidate cultures that are more or less entrepreneurial, more or less customer focused, more or less bureaucratic. In egregious cases where people feel considerably alienated from the culture of their organization, they may vote with their feet and leave. This is rare, however, especially among BritArm employees, many of whom opine that the costs of changing organizations are high and the chances of finding an organization that would both value their skills and have a culture that they would find more desirable low. Instead, cultural democracy is a micro-level process consisting of the continuous stream of small decisions that individuals in the organization make—usually without regard for the impact that those decisions may have on the macro-level pattern of culture, indeed often taken without any conscious thought at all—about what to do, what to say, what to think.

The analogy to popular culture is clear. Writing of the spread of American popular culture across the globe and the anti-American sentiment that has seemed to spread with it, Salman Rushdie has noted: "In most people's heads, globalization has come to mean the worldwide triumph of Nike, the Gap and MTV. Confusingly, we want these goods and services when we behave as consumers, but with our cultural hats on we have begun to deplore their omnipresence" (Rushdie 1999, 6). The same phenomenon can be seen in the United States: as consumers we produce the very patterns of culture that as lay ethnographers we may deplore. There need be no inconsistency: we may genuinely regret the dumbing down of American culture while nevertheless finding ourselves at the cinema enjoying Hollywood's latest blockbuster; or we may find ourselves agreeing so passionately with a *New York Times* op-ed piece arguing that American culture has become too generic and too corporatist that we spill our Starbucks® Mocha Frappuccino® right down the front of our Gap T-shirt, soaking the large letters of its logo.

This should not be confusing. It is an extension of Giddens's formula: "Human history is created by intentional activities but is not an intended project; it persistently eludes efforts to bring it under conscious direction" (Giddens 1984, 27). Absent collective action, our individual choices about what to do, what to eat, what to wear, have but a minuscule impact on the overall pattern of culture. So minuscule, indeed, that it is easy for us to overlook altogether the sense in which we are active in culture's reproduction and to see culture in reified terms as something—some thing—that we have inherited. Furthermore, given the constraints of choice that we face and the particular costs and benefits that the current culture affords various actions, it may make perfect sense to behave as we do even if we *do* understand that this behavior has the cumulative effect of reproducing the culture that we complain about (see Schelling [1978]). Perhaps the more we realize this complicity in ourselves, the louder we feel compelled to complain in order somehow to absolve ourselves of the guilt of what, in tiny measure, we have helped create.

This is the dilemma of cultural democracy, and it is why it should come as no surprise that there is so little connection in BritArm between complaint about the culture and changes to it. The rules in the Bank about the need for tact and discretion and for avoiding embarrassment—rules that include knowledge about when they may be bent and how they may be broken—tend to neuter complaint by channeling it in directions where it will have the least impact on whatever is being complained about. Furthermore, complaint about the Bank serves as a way of euphemizing the exercise of power, of denying responsibility for decisions and actions that specifically reinforce unpopular elements of the current culture. When such decisions are cast, not as the result of conscious choice, but as the necessary, if unfortunate, result of well-known flaws of the Bank and its culture, managers are able to complain about the new policies even as they implement them. Employees are wise to the disguise.

Recall the comment of a doer 2 reported in chapter 2: "That's the culture. Everything is bad news. Otherwise they'd have to pay us more." The point of euphemism is politeness and apparent decency, not deceit. Finally, as well as disguising purposeful action, complaint can disguise its absence. As we saw in chapter 5, complaint can serve as a subterfuge, masking inaction while insulating the complainer from charges of complacency about the culture.

Nevertheless, some of the negativity in the Bank about the culture *is* designed to inspire the collective action needed for change. To achieve this, it is necessary to break the normal rules of polite and legitimate complaint. You must complain in ways that, by definition, are considered illegitimate, heretical. And you must be loud. Because complaining about the Bank fills so many different and useful roles in the culture, there is a lot of it around; to be heard over the din of this constant chatter, it is necessary to speak in a raised voice. As we saw in chapter 5, however, there is a fine line between complaining loudly enough to avoid being ignored as innocuous and complaining so loudly as to be rejected as rude and ignorant. Equally, it is a tricky balancing act to demonstrate with your words and actions a sufficient understanding of the culture's norms to avoid being dismissed as naive—or as an outsider—while not inadvertently reinforcing with those words and actions the very elements of the culture that you hope to change and having your complaint seen as one more effort at polite bonding or blaming. The ironic result of the large amount of complaining that goes on in the Bank is that it makes complaining in a way that might lead to change more difficult. Overall, the complaints about the Bank serve best those who wish it changed least.

LAY ETHNOGRAPHY AS SOCIAL COMMENTARY

To those of us who are not part of the Bank, who do not figure in its political maneuverings, and who are not players in its language games, the lay ethnography in BritArm is more revealing in what it *displays* about the organization's culture than in what it explicitly *says*. This is because the unwritten rules of legitimate lay ethnography in the Bank not only constrain action; they constrain description as well. I have discussed at length the ways in which, on the one hand, the need to complain about the Bank in order to fit in and to avoid being seen as either complacent about the Bank's culture or as strangely enthusiastic about it and, on the other, the shared sentiments about what constitutes a valid and appropriate complaint constrain the sorts of judgments typically heard about the culture. But this is not the only constraint on the Bank's lay ethnographers. The strictures of tact and discretion, the strong aversion to embarrassment, and the fact that the subject and the audience of lay ethnography are one and the same create for lay ethnographers what we might call *Boswell's dilemma*.

James Boswell (1740–95) is the author of what is widely considered to be the finest biography in the English language, the *Life of Johnson* (1791). Boswell spent the best years of his life preparing to write this biography of his friend and idol Samuel Johnson and took seven years after Johnson's death to finish it, missing deadline after deadline and almost abandoning the project in despair. The book is remarkable for three things. First, as Boswell's own biographer, Adam Sisman (2000) notes, it introduced what was seen then as the startling innovation (particularly striking in its contrast to Johnson's own biographical style) of trying to portray its subject "as he really was," describing Johnson's faults and lapses and weaknesses as well as his great qualities. Second, Boswell began recording Johnson's life before the great man was in his grave. Boswell kept a record of Johnson's conversations whenever he was present by taking brief notes as soon as possible afterward and then reconstructing them in full later in his copious journals. Johnson, a turgid writer whose own works are seldom still read, proved to be an eminently quotable conversationalist. Third, insisting that "minute particulars are frequently characterisck, and always amusing, when they relate to a distinguished man" (Boswell [1791] 1934–50, 20), Boswell recorded the smallest details of Johnson's life: what he ate; what he wore; how he behaved. In so doing, he brings to life for the reader, not just the man, but his times. Boswell is the biographer as field-worker, even ethnographer.

Lay ethnographer, that is, for the world evoked by Boswell was his own world and that of his immediate audience. Many of Johnson's interlocutors in the private conversations described so publicly by Boswell were still alive when the book was published. The book was an immediate and enduring success. At the time of its publication, however, Boswell was ridiculed for the level of seemingly insignificant detail that he provided. He was scolded by a scandalized—but titillated—audience for the intimate and unflattering revelations that he offered about Johnson's life. The *Life* was also faulted because it portrayed Johnson as neither great scholar nor consummate scoundrel but rather as the complicated human being that he was. Most painfully for Boswell, an intensely social man, he found himself mistrusted and, therefore, excluded from much of good society for—as one aggrieved associate of Johnson's who was embarrassed by passages in *Life of Johnson* that showed him being mocked merciless by that man put it—"his violating the primary law of civil society in publishing in that work men's unreserved correspondence and unguarded conversation" (Thomas Percy quoted in Sisman 2000, 285). As the reputation of the book continued to rise, the reputation of its author fell further and further. Boswell died only four years after the publication of the book, a drunken and disappointed man.

For over a century after his death, the received wisdom about Boswell and his biography was formed by a highly influential review written by the essayist and historian Thomas Macaulay that appeared in the September 1831 *Edinburgh Review*. Macaulay praised the book while depreciating the man:

> The Life of Johnson is assuredly a great, a very great work. Homer is not more decidedly the first of heroic poets, Shakespeare is not more decidedly the first of dramatists, Demosthenes is not more decidedly the first of orators, than Boswell is the first of biographers. He has no second. He has distanced all his competitors so decidedly that it is not worth while to place them. Eclipse is first, and the rest nowhere.
>
> We are not sure that there is in the whole history of the human intellect so strange a phenomenon as this book. Many of the greatest men that ever lived have written biography. Boswell was one of the smallest men that ever lived, and he has beaten them all. (Macaulay 1831, 16)

What is especially interesting is that Macaulay goes on to claim that the book was so great, not *in spite* of Boswell's weaknesses, but exactly *because* of them:

> Without all the qualities which made him the jest and the torment of those among whom he lived, without the officiousness, the inquisitiveness, the effrontery, the toad-eating, the insensibility to all reproof he never could have produced so excellent a book. He was a slave, proud of his servitude, a Paul Pry, convinced that his own curiosity and garrulity were virtues, an unsafe companion who never scrupled to repay the most liberal hospitality by the basest violation of confidence, a man without delicacy, without shame, without sense enough to know when he was hurting the feelings of others or when he was exposing himself to derision; and because he was all this, he has, in an important department of literature, immeasurably surpassed such writers as Tacitus, Clarendon, Alfieri, and his own idol Johnson. (18)

The very qualities that made Boswell such a good ethnographic biographer, and that give his *Life of Johnson* currency two centuries later, were those that earned him such social reproof and disrespect for so long. These are, first, his willingness to appear naive and to ask dumb questions—"stirring," as he put it, to create good copy for his notes (Sisman 2000, 118). Next, his careful note taking (recording the exact details that he observed), his ability faithfully to reconstruct conversations from his notes, and his temerity in publishing those reconstructed conversations. And, perhaps most of all, his ability to make the events and personages described come through so clearly that it is easy to overlook the artifice, the careful skill that we now know—following the discovery earlier this century of thousands of pages of his notes—went into his writing and to mistake Boswell for a mere stenographer, somehow always in the right place at the right time, who simply recorded what he saw and heard.

This is Boswell's dilemma. Fieldwork and ethnography by their very nature violate common norms of self-presentation, tact, and discretion. It is the task of ethnography to make explicit what normally goes unsaid, to belabor what is obvious to those whom we are studying, to make people feel comfortable around us and then watch them and listen and have the temerity to repeat in public what we think we have seen and heard. Not just in BritArm is this a bad way to win friends and influence people. Not for nothing do field-workers represent themselves as, at best, "marginal natives" (Freilich 1970). Few ethnographers of any persuasion can live up to the example that Boswell has set for us. Done to the standards of ordained ethnography, lay ethnography could never have the ability to warm up conversations in the Bank, strengthen social bonds, conveniently shift blame, or politely euphemize power. Thus, the lay ethnography in BritArm typically, and of necessity, falls short of this standard. Even among those informants who, in private, described elements of the culture to me in trenchant terms, it is formulaic, clichéd, patterned, politically correct in its public form. It picks up and repeats the hackneyed phrasings of organizational culture self-help manuals given authority by virtue of their being recycled in the business press.

This should not be taken as criticism: in this way does lay ethnography best fulfill its important roles within the Bank's culture. But it is why we learn less about the culture from what the lay ethnography says—about the culture being bureaucratic, inflexible, not customer focused, and so on—than from what it displays. From the symmetries in who complains (for, in BritArm, lay ethnography inevitably takes the form of complaint about the culture) about what to whom, we learn about the boundaries of group identity in the Bank's lumpy landscape of overlapping subcultures. From the asymmetries in the complaint, we learn about positioning in the organization's status hierarchy. From the complaints conspicuously not being made publicly, we learn what is taboo in the culture. That is what this book has sought to accomplish: to expose and explain from observations of the ways in which people in the Bank complain about their culture, and the way in which other people in the Bank react to those complaints, the rules and roles, the causes and effects, of lay ethnography and, in so doing, help us better understand how the organization works.

Ethnography as Cultural Critique

George Marcus and Michael Fischer (1986) have famously argued that the role of anthropology and its method, ethnography, in the modern world should be as a source of cultural critique back home. They write: "What has propelled many modern anthropologists into the field and motivated resultant ethnographic accounts is a desire to enlighten their readers about other ways of life, but often with the aim of disturbing their cultural self-satisfaction. Thus, as they have written detailed descriptions and analyses of other cultures, ethnographers have simultaneously had a marginal or hidden agenda of critique of their own culture, namely, the bourgeois, middle-class life of mass liberal societies, which industrial capitalism has produced" (Marcus and Fischer 1986, 111). Yet, the authors note, the promise of anthropology as a compelling form of cultural critique has remained largely unfulfilled. Given what we see in BritArm, this is perhaps not surprising. Industrial capitalism has co-opted the genre of ethnography as cultural critique and repackaged it for sale in the booming trade of business books. This is just one sign that complaint about modern culture has become so common as to form a legitimate part of the popular culture that it seeks to critique. There is plenty of cultural criticism about; it is just that not much of it compels us to action. As Robert Hughes argues in *Culture of Complaint* (1993), never has there been so much complaint about the culture, and never has that complaint seemed so innocuous or bourgeois culture more resilient.

The result is that it has become harder for anthropological or sociological critique with genuinely revolutionary aims to be heard above the din. To distinguish itself, it has sometimes turned heretical and aimed to shock, like Said's (1978) *Orientalism*. But, in so doing, its polemics risk closing the ears of those whom the critique most needs to reach if change is to occur. In other cases, it has retreated into an obscurity of prose and experimentality of method extreme enough that it can have moral force only among the select few who already agree with its political and theoretical assumptions sufficiently to understand it. As criticizing the culture becomes more popular, even de rigueur, the ordained critics of culture risk becoming marginalized, their voices muted.

BritArm is one British bank. It is not a microcosm of broader British society, let alone American society. But neither is it unique in its unpopular culture. It stands as a reminder that cultural critique serves many cultural purposes, most of them unrelated or even antithetical to the change that the critique ostensibly calls for. And it stands as a reminder too that sometimes, to make sense of things, what we need is not more ethnography *as* cultural critique but more ethnography *of* cultural critique. Marshall Sahlins writes: "'Culture'—the word itself or some local equivalent—is on everyone's lips. Tibetans and Hawaiians, Ojibway, Kwakiutl and Eskimo, Kazakhs and Mongols, native Australians, Balinese, Kashmiris and New Zealand Maori: all now discover they have a 'culture.' For centuries they may hardly have noticed it" (Sahlins 1994, 378). We can add to that list the denizens of corporate Britain and America and perhaps learn something from them about the wider impact of anthropology's great gift to the world's mass market: *culture.*

References

PRIMARY SOURCES

Allaire, Y., and M. E. Firsirotu. 1984. Theories of organizational culture. *Organization Studies* 5 (3): 193–226.

Alvesson, Mats. 1993. *Cultural perspectives on organizations.* Cambridge: Cambridge University Press.

Anderson, Gregory. 1976. *Victorian clerks.* Manchester: Manchester University Press.

Argyris, Chris. 1954. *Organization of a bank.* New Haven, Conn.: Yale University, Labor and Management Center.

Austin, J. 1961. A plea for excuses. In *Philosophical papers,* ed. J. D. Urmson and G. Warnock, 123–52. Oxford: Clarendon.

Baba, Marietta L. 1989. Organizational culture: Revisiting the small-society metaphor. *Anthropology of Work Review* 10:7–10.

Barley, Stephen R. 1983. Semiotics and the study of occupational and organizational cultures. *Administrative Science Quarterly* 28 (3): 393–413.

Barley, Stephen R., Gordon W. Meyer, and Debra C. Gash. 1988. Cultures of culture: Academics, practitioners, and the pragmatics of normative control. *Administrative Science Quarterly* 33 (1): 24–60.

Barnes, Julian. 1985. *Flaubert's parrot.* New York: Vintage.

Becker, Howard. 1997. *Outsiders: Studies in the sociology of deviance.* New York: Simon & Schuster.

Benoit, William. 1995. *Accounts, excuses, and apologies: A theory of image restoration strategies.* Albany: State University of New York Press.

Berger, Bennett M. 1995. *An essay on culture: Symbolic structure and social structure.* Berkeley and Los Angeles: University of California Press.

Berger, Peter L., and Thomas Luckmann. 1967. *The social construction of reality.* New York: Doubleday.

Bosk, Charles L. 1992. *All God's mistakes: Genetic counseling in a pediatric hospital.* Chicago: University of Chicago Press.

Boswell, James. [1791] 1934–50. *Life of Johnson*. Oxford: Oxford University Press.

Bourdieu, Pierre. 1984. *Distinction: A social critique of the judgment of taste*. Cambridge, Mass.: Harvard University Press.

———. 1990. *The logic of practice*. Stanford, Calif.: Stanford University Press.

Bourdieu, Pierre, and Loïc J. D. Wacquant. 1992. *An invitation to reflexive sociology*. Chicago: University of Chicago Press.

Burawoy, Michael. 1979. *Manufacturing consent: Changes in the labor process under monopoly capitalism*. Chicago: University of Chicago Press.

Clausen, Christopher. 1996. Welcome to post-culturalism. *American Scholar* 65:379–88.

Clayman, Michelle. 1987. In search of excellence: The investor's viewpoint. *Financial Analysts Journal* 33:54–63.

Clifford, James, and George E. Marcus. 1986. *Writing culture: The poetics and politics of ethnography*. Berkeley and Los Angeles: University of California Press.

Collins, James C., and Jerry I. Porras. 1994. *Built to last: Successful habits of visionary companies*. New York: Harper Business.

Crozier, Michel. 1964. *The bureaucratic phenomenon*. Chicago: University of Chicago Press.

Dalton, Melville. 1959. *Men who manage: Fusions of feeling and theory in administration*. New York: Wiley.

Evans-Pritchard, Edward E. 1940. *The Nuer*. Oxford: Oxford University Press.

Fowler, H. W. 1965. *A dictionary of modern English usage*. Oxford: Oxford University Press.

Freilich, Morris. 1970. *Marginal natives*. New York: Wiley.

Gans, Herbert J. [1974] 1999. *Popular culture and high culture*. Rev. and updated ed. New York: Basic.

Geertz, Clifford. 1973a. Deep play: Notes on the Balinese cockfight. In *The interpretation of cultures*, 412–53. New York: Basic.

———. 1973b. Thick description: Toward an interpretive theory of culture. In *The interpretation of cultures*, 3–30. New York: Basic.

———. 2000. *Available light: Anthropological reflections on philosophical topics*. Princeton, N.J.: Princeton University Press.

Giddens, Anthony. 1984. *The constitution of society*. Berkeley and Los Angeles: University of California Press.

Goffman, Erving. 1961a. *Asylums: Essays on the social situation of mental patients and other inmates*. New York: Doubleday.

———. 1961b. *Encounters: Two studies in the sociology of interaction*. Indianapolis: Bobbs-Merrill.

———. 1974. *Frame analysis: An essay on the organization of experience*. Boston: Northeastern University Press.

Gusfeld, Joseph. 1981. *The culture of public problems*. Chicago: University of Chicago Press.

Hannerz, Ulf. 1992. *Cultural complexity: Studies in the social organization of meaning*. New York: Columbia University Press.

Hax, Arnoldo C., and Dean L. Wilde. 1999. The delta model: Adaptive management for a changing world. *Sloan Management Review* 30 (2): 11–28.

Hughes, Everett C. 1961. *Students' culture and perspectives*. Lawrence: University of Kansas School of Law.

Hughes, Robert. 1993. *Culture of complaint: A passionate look into the ailing heart of America*. New York: Warner.

Humphreys, L. 1970. *Tea room trade: A study of homosexual encounters in public places.* Chicago: Aldine.

Jackall, Robert. 1978. *Workers in a labyrinth: Jobs and survival in a bank bureaucracy.* New York: Universe.

————. 1988. *Moral mazes: The world of corporate managers.* Oxford: Oxford University Press.

Jacques, E. 1951. *The changing culture of a factory.* London: Tavistock Institute.

Jordon, Ann T. 1989. Organizational culture: It's here, but is it anthropology? *Anthropology of Work Review* 10 (3): 2–5.

Keesing, Roger M. 1974. Theories of culture. *Annual Review of Anthropology* 3:73–97.

Kilmann, Ralph H. 1985. Five steps for closing culture-gaps. In *Gaining control of the corporate culture,* ed. R. H. Kilmann, M. J. Saxton, R. Serpa, et al., 351–69. San Francisco: Jossey-Bass.

Kroeber, Alfred L., and C. Kluckhohn. 1952. *Culture: A critical review of concepts and definitions.* Cambridge, Mass.: Harvard University Press.

Kunda, Gideon. 1992. *Engineering culture: Control and commitment in a high-tech corporation.* Philadelphia: Temple University Press.

Lamont, Michele. 1992. *Money, morals, and manners: The culture of the French and the American upper-middle class.* Chicago: University of Chicago Press.

Latour, Bruno. 1996. *Aramis; or, The love of technology.* Cambridge, Mass.: Harvard University Press.

Lyman, Stanford M., and Marvin B. Scott. 1970. *A sociology of the absurd.* New York: Appleton Century Crofts.

Macaulay, Thomas. 1831. Review of *The Life of Johnson. Edinburgh Review,* September, pp. 16–18.

Malinowski, Bronislaw. [1922] 1961. *Argonauts of the western Pacific.* New York: Dutton.

Marcus, George E., and Michael M. J. Fischer. 1986. *Anthropology as cultural critique: An experimental moment in the human sciences.* Chicago: University of Chicago Press.

Martin, Joanne. 1992. *Cultures in organizations: Three perspectives.* Oxford: Oxford University Press.

Martin, Joanne, and Debra Meyerson. 1988. Organizational cultures and the denial, channeling, and acknowledgment of ambiguity. In *Managing ambiguity and change,* ed. L. R. Pondy, J. Boland, J. Richard, and H. Thomas, 93–125. New York: Wiley.

McArthur, Tom. 1992. *The Oxford companion to the English language.* Oxford: Oxford University Press.

Meek, V. Lynn. 1988. Organizational culture: Origins and weaknesses. *Organization Studies* 9 (4): 453–73.

Micklethwait, John, and Adrian Wooldridge. 1996. *The witch doctors: Making sense of the management gurus.* New York: Random House.

Mukerji, Chandra, and Michael Schudson. 1986. Popular culture. *Annual Review of Sociology* 12:47–66.

Neuhauser, Peg, Ray Bender, and Kirk Stromberg. 2000. *Culture.com: Building corporate culture in the connected workplace.* New York: Wiley.

Ouchi, William G. 1981. *Theory Z: How American businesses can meet the Japanese challenges.* Reading, Mass.: Addison-Wesley.

Paramount Communications, Inc. v. Time, Inc. 1989. Fed. Sec. L. Rep. (CCH) P94, 514 (Del. Ch.). LEXIS 77, *1–*90.

Paxman, Jeremy. 1998. *The English: A portrait of a people*. London: Penguin.

Perlow, Leslie. 1997. *Finding time: How corporations, individuals, and families can benefit from new work practices*. Ithaca, N.Y.: ILR Press.

Perrow, Charles. 1984. *Normal accidents: Living with high-risk technologies*. New York: Basic.

———. 1986. *Complex organizations: A critical essay*. 3d ed. New York: McGraw-Hill.

Peters, Thomas J., and Robert H. Waterman. 1982. *In Search of excellence: Lessons from America's best-run companies*. New York: Harper & Row.

Ramanujam, V., and N. Venkatraman. 1988. Excellence, planning, and performance. *Interfaces* 18 (3): 23–31.

Rohlen, Thomas P. 1974. *For harmony and strength: Japanese white-collar organization in anthropological perspective*. Berkeley: University of California Press.

Rosaldo, Renato. 1989. *Culture and truth: The remaking of social analysis*. Boston: Beacon.

Roy, Donald F. 1959–60. "Banana time": Job satisfaction and informal interaction. *Human Organization* 18:158–68.

Sahlins, Marshall. 1994. Goodbye to tristes tropes: Ethnography in the context of modern world history. In *Assessing cultural anthropology*, ed. R. Borofsky, 377–95. New York: McGraw-Hill.

Said, Edward. 1978. *Orientalism*. New York: Vintage.

Schein, Edgar H. 1961. *Coercive persuasion*. New York: Norton.

———. 1991. What is culture? In *Reframing organizational culture*, edited by P. J. Frost, L. F. Moore, M. R. Louis, C. C. Lundberg, and J. Martin, 243–53. Newbury Park, Calif.: Sage.

———. 1992. *Organizational culture and leadership*. 2d ed. San Francisco: Jossey-Bass.

Schelling, Thomas C. 1978. *Micromotives and macrobehavior*. New York: Norton.

Schroder, H. M., A. P. Cockerill, and John W. Hunt. 1993. Validation study into the high performance managerial competencies. Working paper. London: London Business School.

Senge, Peter M. 1990. *The fifth discipline: The art and practice of the learning organization*. New York: Doubleday.

Sisman, Adam. 2000. *Boswell's presumptuous task*. London: Hamish Hamilton.

Smith, Vicki. 1990. *Managing in the corporate interest: Control and resistance in an American bank*. Berkeley and Los Angeles: University of California Press.

Sutton, Robert I. 1991. Maintaining norms about expressed emotions: The case of bill collectors. *Academy of Management Journal* 36:245–68.

Traube, Elizabeth G. 1996. "The popular" in American culture. *Annual Review of Anthropology* 25:127–51.

Van Maanen, John. 1975. Police socialization: A longitudinal examination of job attitudes in an urban police department. *Administrative Science Quarterly* 20 (2): 207–28.

———. 1984. Doing new things in old ways: The chains of socialization. In *College and university organization*, ed. J. L. Bess, 211–47. New York: New York University Press.

———. 1988. *Tales of the field: On writing ethnography*. Chicago: University of Chicago Press.

———. 1991. The smile factory: Work at Disneyland. In *Reframing organizational culture*, ed. P. J. Frost, L. F. Moore, M. R. Louis, C. C. Lundberg, and J. Martin, 58–76. Newbury Park, Calif.: Sage.

Van Maanen, John, and Steve Barley. 1984. Occupational communities. *Research in Organizational Behavior* 6:287–364.

Van Maanen, John, and Gideon Kunda. 1989. Real feelings: Emotional expression and organizational culture. In *Research in organizational behavior*, ed. B. M. Staw and L. L. Cummings, 43–103. Greenwich, Conn.: JAI.

Weber, Max. 1978. *Economy and society: An outline of interpretive sociology.* Berkeley and Los Angeles: University of California Press.

Whyte, William Foote. 1955. *Street corner society: The social structure of an Italian slum.* Chicago: University of Chicago Press.

Whyte, William H. 1956. *The organization man.* New York: Doubleday.

Willis, Paul. 1977. *Learning to labor: How working class kids get working class jobs.* New York: Columbia University Press.

Wilson, Sloan. 1955. *The man in the gray flannel suit.* New York: Simon & Schuster.

Wittgenstein, Ludwig. 1958. *Philosophical investigations.* Translated by G. E. M. Anscombe. 3d ed. New York: Macmillan.

Young, Ed. 1991. On the naming of the rose: Interests and multiple meanings as elements of organizational culture. In *Reframing organizational culture*, ed. P. J. Frost, L. F. Moore, M. R. Louis, C. C. Lundberg, and J. Martin, 90–103. Newbury Park, Calif.: Sage.

NEWSPAPER AND MAGAZINE ARTICLES

Activate the money star. 1997. *Economist*, 3 May, 66.

AOL, CompuServe shares jump on idea of takeover. 1997. *Wall Street Journal*, 2 April, B7.

As in-your-face ads backfire, Nike finds a new global tack. 1997. *Wall Street Journal*, 5 May, A1.

At ABB, globalization isn't just a buzzword: It's a corporate culture. 1996. *Wall Street Journal*, 1 October, A1.

Back on top? A survey of American business. 1995. *Economist*, 16 September, 15.

Bean-counters unite. 1997. *Economist*, 25 October, 77.

The big cheese who plans to come to the rescue at M&S. 2000. *The Times*, 25 January, 29.

Bill Clinton? He was president in the Goizueta era. 1997. *Wall Street Journal*, 24 October, A22.

Boom and gloom in Germany. 1997. *Economist*, 5 April, 72.

BT vaults into ranks of telecom titans by moving to buy MCI. 1996. *Wall Street Journal*, 4 November, A1.

Cause for ConCERN? 2000. *Economist*, 28 October, 112.

CEO to go. 2000. *Economist*, 9 December, 91.

The changing nature of leadership. 1995. *Economist*, 10 June, 57.

Chrysler-Daimler has little overlap, prompting label of a "dream team." 1998. *Wall Street Journal*, 7 May, B1.

Commercial propositions. 1998. *Economist*, 5 December, 101.

Coopers, Price Waterhouse plan merger worth about $12 billion. 1997. *Wall Street Journal*, 19 September, A3.

Cordiant picks agency novice to steer Saatchi & Saatchi. 1997. *Wall Street Journal*, 5 May, B5.

The DaimlerChrysler emulsion. 2000. *Economist*, 29 July, 69–70.

The decline and fall of General Motors. 1998. *Economist*, 10 October, 69.

Deutsche's wayward wunderkind. 1996. *Economist*, 14 September, 86.

Doing it differently. 1997. *Economist*, 19 April, 73.

Doing the right thing. 1995. *Economist*, 20 May, 64.

Dons and dollars. 1996. *Economist*, 20 July, 53.

Dusting the opposition. 1995. *Economist*, 29 April, 72.

EDS unit's bid for Kearney may create a culture clash. 1995. *Wall Street Journal*, 5 May, B1.

Engineering dominance. 1995. *Economist*, 22 July, 64.

Ernst blamed for collapse of merger. 1998. *Wall Street Journal*, 17 February, A3.

Europe's businesses, yearning to breathe free. 1997. *Economist*, 2 August, 52.

Ever so polite. 2001. *Economist*, 17 February, 69.

Fatal attraction. 1996. *Economist*, 23 March, 73–74.

Flattering to deceive. 2001. *Economist*, 4 August, 13.

Food for thought. 1999. *Economist*, 10 July, 76.

Furnishing the world. 1994. *Economist*, 19 November, 102.

Gadget wars. 2001. *Economist*, 10 March, 67.

German lessons. 1997. *Economist*, 18 October, 89.

A great leap, preferably forward. 2001. *Economist*, 20 January, 69.

How a chemicals giant goes about becoming a lot less German. 1997. *Wall Street Journal*, 18 February, A1.

How Delta's pilots mobilized against management. 2001. *Wall Street Journal*, 24 April, A1.

Hydrophobia. 1997. *Economist*, 23 August, 51.

Inside the empire of Exxon the unloved. 1994. *Economist*, 5 March, 69.

Insular culture helped Yahoo! grow, but has now hurt it in the long run. 2001. *Wall Street Journal*, 9 March, A1.

Is this Europe's best bank? 2002. *BusinessWeek*, 29 July, 32.

It ain't necessarily so. 1998. *Economist*, 17 October, 81.

Jager's gamble. 1999. *Economist*, 30 October, 85.

The kingdom inside a republic. 1996. *Economist*, 13 April, 66–67.

Korean Air tries to fix a dismal safety record. 1999. *Wall Street Journal*, 7 July, A1.

Lawyers go global. 2000. *Economist*, 26 February, 93.

Lennar thrives as oddball culture helps to tie home builder together. 2001. *Wall Street Journal*, 27 July, A1.

The Lex column: The price of delay. 1994. *Financial Times*, 3 August, 16.

Love me. 2002. *Economist*, 23 February, 42.

Lufthansa is waking up to need for global alliances. 1997. *Wall Street Journal Europe*, 15 September, A1.

Many new executives are being discharged with stunning speed. 1994. *Wall Street Journal*, 4 March, A1.

Mobile warfare. 1999. *Economist*, 20 November, 16.

A modern Don Quixote still tilts at headquarters. 1998. *Wall Street Journal*, 28 January, CA1.

Mogul Reinhard Mohn leads Bertelsmann far from the media crowd. 1997. *Wall Street Journal*, 14 January, A1.

Mr. Davies's NewROses. 1997. *Economist*, 4 October, 93.

New formula Coke. 2001. *Economist*, 3 February, 76.

No smoking please, we're British. 1992. *The Times*, 7 August, 3.

Off with their beards. 2001. *Economist*, 2 June, 74.

Palace coup. 1999. *Economist*, 16 January, 70.

Pearson pins hopes for big turnaround on American woman. 1996. *Wall Street Journal*, 18–19 October, A1.

Pepsi challenge: Can company's brass mute flashy culture and make profits fizz? 1997. *Wall Street Journal*, 8 August, A1.

Philip Morris's passion to market cigarettes helps it outsell RJR. 1995. *Wall Street Journal*, 30 October, A1.

Piggy banks. 1994. *Daily Mirror*, 3 August, 6.

Play nicely, or not at all. 1998. *Economist*, 23 May, 21.

Promodes ups the stakes in casino takeover fight. 1997. *Wall Street Journal*, 26 September, A18.

Real-estate merger wave hits third-generation family firm. 1997. *Wall Street Journal*, 25 April, B14.

Rebuilding the garage. 2000. *Economist*, 15 July, 63.

Ridding Russia of Taylor-made businesses. 1996. *Wall Street Journal*, 23 September, A12.

Ripe for picking. 1999. *Economist*, 5 August, 46.

Rubbermaid tries to regain lost stature. 1995. *Wall Street Journal*, 6 December, B1.

Rushdie, Salman. 1999. Sneakers and burgers aren't the real enemies. *International Herald Tribune*, 6–7 March, 6.

Salomon succumbs at last. 1997. *Economist*, 27 September, 82.

The shape of phones to come. 2001. *Economist*, 24 March, 22.

The shape of the battle ahead. 2000. *Economist*, 18 November, 36.

Some companies cut costs too far, suffer "corporate anorexia." 1995. *Wall Street Journal*, 5 July, A1.

To avoid a job failure, learn the culture of a company first. 1998. *Wall Street Journal*, 14 July, B1.

To the Finland base station. 1999. *Economist*, 9 October, 27.

Try, try again. 2000. *Economist*, 8 April, 74.

Unthinking shrinking. 1995. *Economist*, 9 September, 70.

Wasserstein unit to buy publisher of law journals. 1997. *Wall Street Journal*, 24 October, B8.

Weisel's quitting NationsBank prompts a "what went wrong"? 1998. *Wall Street Journal*, 22 September, C1.

What next? 2000. *Economist*, 12 February, 72.

What price success for a newly popular BBC? 2002. *International Herald Tribune*, 6 February, 18.

Why AT&T takeover of NCR hasn't been a real bell ringer. 1995. *Wall Street Journal*, 19 September, A1.

Why too many mergers miss the mark. 1997. *Economist*, 4 January, 61.

World Bank's new emphasis focuses on results, culture. 1997. *Asian Wall Street Journal*, 8 September, A1.

Worldbeater, Inc. 1997. *Economist*, 22 November, 108.

You're in the army now—the one with the golden arches. 1995. *Wall Street Journal*, 19 December, A19.

Index